Close Relationships

Close Relationships

PERSPECTIVES

ON THE

MEANING OF INTIMACY

Edited by George Levinger & Harold L. Raush

University of Massachusetts Press
Amherst 1977

Library of Congress Cataloging in Publication Data
appear on the last printed page of this book.

An abbreviated version of "Private Lives and Public Order,"
by Howard Gadlin, originally appeared
in Volume XVII, No. 2 of *The Massachusetts Review,*
copyright © 1976 by *The Massachusetts Review.*

Contents

CONTENTS

Preface

The unproblematic remains unquestioned and uninvestigated. It takes a change, a puzzle, a conflict to call an issue to our attention. Our era's concern with *relationship* reflects that changes—social and economic, as well as personal and interpersonal—are occurring; but are as yet poorly understood. On the one hand, we witness a quest for closeness; on the other hand, there is a breakup and distancing. Certainly, traditional concepts of relationship are under question.

We are no longer sure of the meaning of such words as friendship, marriage, love, intimacy, family, closeness, or distance; the boundaries that once seemed to define such concepts have become diffuse. The psychological counterpart to this diffusion is uncertainty; not only do our interpersonal relationships come under examination, but also we are less certain about what is right or wrong, good or bad, or, in present-day jargon, healthy or pathological.

The close relationship—friendship, kinship, erotic love—is obviously not new. Interpersonal attachment, loyalty, and commitment in the face of conflict have long been universal themes. How strange, then, that social science comes so late to examine such relationships. A partial explanation is that the sciences, including the social sciences, blossomed in a world much different from the present one. That earlier world may appear simple to us, for its changes occurred at a slower rate, and its relationships were embedded in a social structure which lent them more meaning and stability. Although there were deviations from the standards of the time, and although stability was threatened by death and social disruption, relationships among friends, lovers, spouses, and family had their place in a narrowly defined community. Those limits could have been a source of conflict, but the conflict tended to be external—the relationship versus social standards.

It was the individual who was jeopardized by the rapid changes accompanying the technological developments of the nineteenth century. Hero and victim of the process of adaptation, the individual became the primary focus of social science. Psychology studied individual processes—perception, cognition, learning, and socialization; social psychology focused on the effects of social factors on the individual. Sociology and anthropology, while oriented toward broader conceptions—social institutions, demographic variations, roles, rituals, group structures—also sought to explain the impact of social variables on individual experience and behavior. And therapy, as a profession, developed to help discontented individuals make compromises with civilization.

In the first half of the twentieth century a few social scientists, but relatively few, became interested in the interpersonal. Psychologists and sociologists began to study heterosexual attraction and marital stability. The dominant focus, nonetheless, was still on the individual. Psychologists looked for personality variables that attracted (or failed to attract) partners, and searched for the effects of demographic factors on individual behavior. Despite a growing interest in relationships, the relationship itself lacked substance. It was the individual who was assigned an interior life, and the relationship was merely a "dependent variable."

Yet recently, this perception seems to be changing. The individual has become less hero and more victim. He* is faced with increasing contradictions. The ideology emerging in the late nineteenth century gave him the responsibility for choosing his own social and economic life—a responsibility not afforded earlier generations. Moreover, where social democracy holds sway, the individual assumes responsibility for his social institutions. Our recent ideology suggests not only that the forces of nature and human behavior are modifiable by individual action, but also that the individual bears responsibility for such action.

There is, however, a paradox. While expected to control his world, the individual is constantly reminded of his impotence. The media daily inform him of events beyond his control. Increasingly, he has become an anonymous product in a world geared to mass production. As a

*In the following paragraphs, read "he" as *he or she* and "his" as *his or her*.

consumer, he is as "packaged" as the products of the market in which he is an anonymous customer. As a producer, he is a cog in a machine whose complexities are beyond his understanding. Even if he belongs to the fortunate minority who are not alienated from their work, incomprehensible events and massive bureaucracies challenge his control.

Moreover, we witness such a diffusion of social norms that almost "anything goes." We see a decline of community support systems—not only of neighboring kin, but also of modest institutions like the corner grocery or the neighborhood bar. Increased mobility and decreased family size further the individual's isolation.

It is no surprise, then, that the intimate relationship has come to be seen as a refuge—a respite from alienation at one's place of work, from isolation in the community, from the incomprehensibility of technology, and from social anonymity. But the walls of that refuge often crumble under the weight they bear. The reliance on intimacy itself creates new difficulties, and today's partners often carry the further burden of what Rosabeth Kanter has called "the discovery of adulthood": our demand for continuing adult growth and change. Such demands might lead us to wonder more at the continuity of intimate relationships than at their dissolution.

The present volume is a product of a two-day symposium on the study of close relationships, held in Amherst in the late Spring of 1974. The meeting was supported by a generous grant from the Institute of Life Insurance's Social Research Grant Program, under the direction of Dr. Harold Edrich; the Institute is now part of the American Council of Life Insurance in Washington, D.C. Work on the manuscript was facilitated by Grants GS-33641 and BNS 76-02575 from the National Science Foundation.

We sent invitations to our symposium to eighteen people representing a diversity of disciplines—family sociology, social psychology, clinical psychology, family therapy, and cultural anthropology. The response was heartening. Although no honoraria were offered, all but three of those invited promptly agreed to participate; and the three who declined expressed enthusiasm for the symposium. Six participants agreed to write core papers, which were distributed several weeks before the meeting. At the symposium, we invited formal commentaries by discussants who were free to criticize, elaborate on, or depart from the papers. These discussants were Jessie S. Bernard, Nancie L. Gonzalez, Lynn Hoffman, Rosabeth M. Kanter, Robert K. Leik, Harold L. Raush, Alice S. Rossi, Robert G. Ryder, and Robert S. Weiss. An informal discussion among all participants followed each set of commentaries. On the final afternoon two other participants, Reuben Hill and Zick Rubin, reviewed implications of the symposium and presented their own independent analyses. The proceedings of the meeting were recorded and carefully transcribed by Sally Ives. Jack Hewitt provided valuable reactions to the manuscript.

The present volume consists of the six core papers and our two concluding chapters. Although each chapter is concerned with close relationships, the contents range from philosophical analysis to research methodology; the time perspectives range from present to past to future. This diversity—found even within individual chapters—is characteristic of the state of the field. Generally speaking, the first three chapters open broad perspectives, whereas the following three chapters focus on particular topics of research and method. The two final chapters grew from the formal commentaries and the informal discussions at the symposium. They elaborate on what precedes them and also incorporate the discussants' contributions, which were vital in developing our thoughts. Our chapters are intended to further the dialogue and to inspire analysis and research into close relationships.

George Levinger
Harold L. Raush
Amherst, Massachusetts
March 1977

Close Relationships

I

The Embrace of Lives:
Changing and Unchanging

GEORGE LEVINGER

The city of Oslo contains a carefully tended park dedicated entirely to the work of Norway's great sculptor, Gustav Vigeland. Most of Vigeland's sculptures from the second part of his life stand there. Beginning with his original idea of the fountain, ringed by human figures in differing poses ranging from youth to maturity, Vigeland's conception of his large park grew to encompass many interpersonal relations on humanity's road from infancy to old age. In one area, a solitary fetus stands on its head in the middle of a circle of infant figures. Elsewhere, the collection displays experiences and attitudes from childhood and adolescence through young adulthood into maturity and senescence. Hundreds of figures are included; most of them are vitally related to one another, either in pairs or in larger groupings. The figures on different pedestals exhibit a broad variety of relations: encounter, greeting, joy, anger, brutality, and embrace.

Vigeland's figures are naked. He believed in the integrity of the human body. His men, women, and children have universal significance; clothing would obscure fundamental reality. Not all who witness them are enthusiastic about Vigeland's heavy shapes, but his total theme receives general acclaim. His theme is the cycle of human life. All personal poses and interpersonal relations take their place within that context.

Many of Vigeland's sculptures depict human pairs, but his park also contains several larger ensembles. One is a group of giants who hold up the huge bowl of the fountain. His largest ensemble is the monolith, the

massive column of intertwined figures who strive upward into the sky—
displaying Vigeland's own sense of restless, striving humanity.

How is Vigeland's work pertinent to our present topic of close
interpersonal relationships? In at least two ways. Not only did this
solitary genius strip away masks of human pretension, but he cast his
images into the context of the life cycle. His cyclical concept suggests
that relations of the moment are transitory; they are properly
appreciated within the arc of a person's, a pair's, or a community's life
span. Human life and location are transitory, but the cycle itself is
eternal.

In this paper, I seize Vigeland's mood. My aim is to strip to its
fundamentals our view of human relatedness. Today, in a large sector of
the Western world where food and industry are no longer the principal
occupation, the conduct of interpersonal relationships has become a
central but confusing concern. One problem for me here is to separate
essentials from debatables, to locate firm ground from which we can
depart in our speculations.

I want to suggest some basic perspectives before posing questions of
contemporary relevance. In writing this paper, I searched for a set of
fundamental paradoxes that would help to expose current dilemmas.
That I have not yet found those paradoxes may be evidence of the
relativity of human experience. But, at a time when we are being asked
to believe in "modular man" and disposable relationships (Toffler,
1970), I do have a need to confront the contemporary with the eternal.

Basic Facts: Lest We Forget

First Facts
People are born.
They mature.
They grow old.
They die.
We all share the experience of helpless beginning; we are likely to
have a helpless or solitary ending. Our life stretches between these
poles: the point of origin and the certain, though indefinite, point of
termination.

Relationships too begin; they continue; they end.

Second Facts   Between the beginning and the ending, what is there? Personal striving, interpersonal connecting. Individual subsistence and creation. Interpersonal meeting, relating, and departure. Perhaps.

The strong and capable strive and accomplish more than the weak and incapable. Perhaps. The beautiful and loving connect more than the ugly and contemptuous. Perhaps.

Interpersonal storms and calms are second facts. So are problems and their solution.

Second facts are less certain than first facts. The sculptor molds them with less sureness. Facts become probabilities. To be observed by the prudent, to be studied by the student, to be disputed by the contentious. Perhaps.

Later Facts   Out of a welter of certainty and probability, humankind has created its institutions. We share "first facts" and "second facts" with other animals, but "later facts" are produced by us. The tool and the machine are later facts. So are ceremony, commitment, contract, obligation. So are social science and social philosophy. All are later facts.

Mass media are later facts. Culture and culture change are later facts. So is the manifold of all we take for granted today—from the alarm that wakes one in the morning to the nighttime reading by which one nods to sleep.

This paper and this symposium surely are later facts.

Fictions   We live not only through fact but also through fiction. Our images and ideals are fictions, albeit very important for governing our actions and desires. Our symbols, which bind people together through joy or despair, are essential fictions.

The necessity of fictions is beyond dispute. What is debatable is which fictions are essential and which fictions are useless or even dangerous.

Interpretation?   How then can I separate fact from fiction, simplicity from complexity? In the forest of contemporary interpersonal relationships, my own view is obscure. I cannot be sure that I see the trees, let alone the larger forests. I cannot truly distinguish between essence and transition. My own life is limited to one moment of history, my

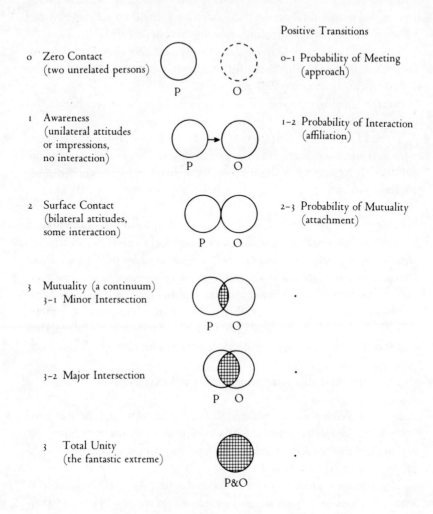

0 Zero Contact
(two unrelated persons)

1 Awareness
(unilateral attitudes
or impressions,
no interaction)

2 Surface Contact
(bilateral attitudes,
some interaction)

3 Mutuality (a continuum)
3-1 Minor Intersection

3-2 Major Intersection

3   Total Unity
(the fantastic extreme)

Positive Transitions

0-1 Probability of Meeting
(approach)

1-2 Probability of Interaction
(affiliation)

2-3 Probability of Mutuality
(attachment)

Figure 1. Levels of pair relationship (from Levinger & Snoek, 1972)

experiences confined to a small corner of the world. My words, then, are a cloudy mixture of early and later facts, and surely fictions. Let me turn to a simple model of pair relationships, which serves as the basis for some researchable questions.

Interpersonal Relations: A View of the Person-Other Pair

Love increases in value . . . as more of the personalities of the people concerned enters into the relation. [Russell, 1929, p. 7]

How are people related to other people?[1] Can we set forth some fundamental distinctions? The least relation is no relation at all—a level of "zero contact" where two people have no awareness whatsoever of each other's existence. This condition is not trivial; it is the reservoir from which spring all further human relations.

Beyond that reservoir, there are three basic levels at which one person can "relate" to another: (1) through one-way observation, without any reciprocation from the other; (2) through two-way interaction, including superficial contacts between either strangers or recurring role partners; and (3) through deeper mutual interdependence, where two persons develop and maintain a unique space of jointness — joint experiences, joint norms, and other mutual properties. From no relation, through unilateral observation and bilateral contact, toward mutuality — these seem to be basic gradations of interpersonal relationship.

Figure 1 conveys the essential distinctions. The topmost pair of circles suggest that at zero contact (Level 0) another individual exists only potentially. At Level 1, a person is oriented toward either an actual or an imagined other, who is viewed from some distance and without benefit of interaction. At Level 2, Person's and Other's lives touch each other in interaction that has outcomes for each of them; such a surface contact is the base point on a continuum of Person-Other mutuality (Level 3), where the relationship may vary from the shallowest to the deepest degrees of interdependence.

[1]This section is based on some of my earlier thinking (cf. Levinger, 1974; Levinger & Snoek, 1972).

Unilateral Awareness (Level 1) The largest portion of one's relations with others consists of momentary impressions of which the perceived other is not aware. In social psychology, the bulk of research on person perception pertains to subject-target encounters where a subject has limited information about a perceived other—frequently about a hypothetical stranger. About such sorts of interpersonal relations we appear to have the most scientific information; yet this is the social relation that probably demands least knowledge. I shall therefore not dwell on this form of Person-Other relation.

Surface Contact (Level 2) A person's reciprocal contacts range from surface into depth, from the trivial meeting to the profound attachment. A surface contact can occur in two ways, either as a transitory first meeting or as a segmental role relation. Transitory meetings take place on street corners, in hallways, at large parties; they also occur in the typical laboratory experiment. One person meets another and receives limited information about him, while also providing limited information to the other about self. Segmental role relations refer to repeated interactions which are guided by the dictates of structured roles.

To the extent that actors in surface contacts play their roles uniquely or elicit unusual interest in one another, surface contacts may lead toward deeper involvements. Some pairs move from role-governed contact toward sharing a more personal relationship. It is difficult, however, to differentiate clearly between interpersonal surface and depth. Much that happens at the beginning is affected by one's anticipation of subsequent developments.

Mutuality (Level 3) The development of mutuality implies the expansion of Person-Other contact beyond that of a transient encounter or one based on externally structured roles (see Levinger & Snoek, 1972). The Person-Other relationship is mutual to the extent that partners possess shared knowledge of each other, care emotionally for each other, assume responsibility for promoting each other's outcomes, and have developed private norms for regulating their association. The bond between their two lives, suggested graphically by the size of the intersections in figure 1, represents the investment and outcomes of the two persons' joint efforts and joint experiences.

It is the cumulation of such investments which best characterizes the essence of a relation*ship*; it is as if they are carried in the "ship" that contains the cargo of each particular human association. Some ships are tiny and flat-bottomed; they drift on the ocean of life, and sink when the seas are disturbed. Other ships are much larger and have deep keels to help stabilize them; they carry a much bigger cargo and some ballast, and they stay afloat in the roughest of seas.

The deep as opposed to the shallow relationship, then, is characterized by stronger communality, heavier emotional investment, and a more definite structure containing it. The support structure can be likened to the hull of a ship and the contents to its cargo.[2]

Interpersonal ships and cargoes The intersection between Person and Other is difficult to define. For the infant and its mother it has to do with touching, warmth, and food; for the mother, it includes seeing the child at rest and contemplating its future. For the child growing up in a family, the attachment to parents and siblings seems to grow; with it goes an increasing store of pleasures and memories, of common experiences that are sometimes treasured. Even negative experiences build the attachment.

In the family, intersections between children and others tend to be communal rather than exclusive. As a person grows up in our culture, however, he or she begins to develop more exclusive relationships. Many friendly relations are casual and can be replaced by almost any other pleasant person. But some friendships become unique partnerships, where the members share in ways they can hardly do with anyone else.

Intimate heterosexual relationships tend to develop still later. The sex act itself is an exclusive union; in some cultures, as in African Kenya, it represents merely a transitory association, but in Middle America it also should imply penetrating social intercourse. In our culture, our closest mature relationship is usually that with a peer of the other sex. There are many exceptions, of course; some unmarried people, for example, live with members of the same sex for as long or longer than the longevity of married couples. The average American child, though, seems to have witnessed a parental relationship that excluded all third

[2]Not all long-lasting relationships or those externally designated as "intimate" are necessarily deep or mutual in my present sense. For example, many marriages or other formal partnerships continue more because of their shells than because of their vital mutuality (Levinger, 1965).

parties from the closest intimacies. That fact alone, which some link with later "oedipal strivings" in our culture (Slater, 1974, p. 113), plays an important part in our socialization process.

Aspects of Person-Other Attachment: Some Questions   Pair relations have been subjected to more research than any other interpersonal relationship, but our knowledge remains primitive. Instead of citing the voluminous but inconclusive literature, I will here pose questions about three aspects of the Person-Other relationship: (1) its *involvement*, which here refers to the size of its intersection; (2) its *commitment*, which pertains to the strength of its boundaries; and (3) its *symmetry*, which refers to the relative equality of the two members' investments and rewards inside and outside the relationship.

Involvement   As Simmel (1908) pointed out long ago, the intimate dyad has a peculiar capacity to involve its members totally; its very size helps to make it the locus of "sentimentalism." Others too have suggested that our most profound attachments, both early and later in life, appear to be dyadic (Bowlby, 1969; Weiss, 1973).

Research on mate selection has so far concentrated on traditional questions, such as the following: What are the determinants of pair formation and involvement? What factors help or hinder the continuation of partnerships in differing cultures or subcultures? One can also raise questions that transcend culture: For instance, how significantly is the longing for intimacy in adulthood linked to the closeness of a child's early family experience? It is widely acknowledged that extreme frustration of infantile attachment is linked to later relational disturbance (e.g., Bowlby, 1969; Harlow, 1958), but we know little about the effects of less extreme conditions.

Other questions pertain to the *content* of deep interpersonal involvement. How, for example, can one improve the vocabulary for talking about such feelings? How can people come to verbalize their liking, loving, and other emotions (cf. Rubin, 1973)? People are inarticulate about interpersonal involvements; they have no explicit language for discussing them. Recent research by my coworkers and me indicates that a person's involvement with another is a composite of several variables: emotional caring for the other, perceived outcome correspondence, mutual disclosure, and the felt uniqueness of the Person-Other relationship. In which relationships, however, and in

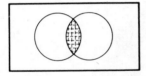 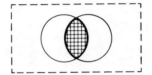

Figure 2. Relationships of (*a*) external restraint and (*b*) internal consent

what societies, is each of those components most salient? Are there other, yet unnamed components, and under what conditions may they become central? How is each component affected by changes in relationships during a person's life span from infancy to old age?

Commitment   Close relationships are held together not only through involvement and care but also through obligations which are either taken on voluntarily by the partners or imposed from outside by society. Two partners' private commitments reflect an informal process that emerges implicitly out of repeated positive interactions; its reward is mutual reciprocation and predictability. Public obligation is imposed by social norms that are subscribed to by both members of a relationship. Despite some insightful writing on interpersonal commitment (e.g., Kanter, 1972; McCall & Simmons, 1966), we have hardly any systematic data about its antecedents and consequences.

What, for example, is the covariation between voluntary dyadic commitment and the intensity of external constraints? Figure 2 illustrates two contrasting examples. The relationship on the left side is held together by strong external forces, while that shown at the right is only weakly contained. The intersection in figure 2*a*, however, is rather empty, while that in figure 2*b* is relatively full. Note also the stronger boundaries around the intersection in figure 2*b*. Extreme external pressure would seem to be associated with lower degrees of pair involvement and with lesser degrees of commitment. Complete lack of external pressure, however, should not necessarily increase the voluntariness of commitment; the association is undoubtedly curvilinear, but we know little about its shape. Since close relationships in contemporary culture are generally private relationships, there is little definitive information about processes of commitment and detachment. For example, today's rates of marital breakup are high, but we have few

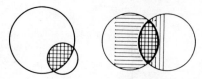

Figure 3. (*left*) A mother-child relationship
Figure 4. (*right*) Asymmetrical involvement between peers

standards for judging the meaning of those rates; it is quite possible, for example, that new commitments being undertaken are markedly sounder than those being dissolved; only the future can tell.

In some quarters today, there is a yearning for ways to escape traditional forms of interpersonal commitment, such as marriage. Yet it is hard to conceive of a relationship that has both depth and continuity without some form of commitment. A major issue in the study of interpersonal relationships pertains to the viability and the risks of varying shapes of interpersonal commitment.

Symmetry The pairs of circles pictured in figure 1 were in each case precisely equal in size. They implied an equality that is rarely attained in reality, where the lives outside the Person-Other intersection tend to be rather different. In the real world, one member's resources or rewards are surpassed by the other's; one partner is more and the other is less dependent on the relationship. A young child's life may be contained almost entirely within the larger circle of the mother's current experience; a husband's and a wife's experiences inside and outside the joint area of their marriage may differ vastly in scope. To the extent that one partner has more alternatives outside the relationship than the other partner, then that relationship is asymmetrical.

Indeed, most interpersonal relations are markedly asymmetrical, including those at either end of the life span and most work associations. But while work relations and the bulk of casual social contacts tend toward inequality, increasing degrees of involvement seem likely to promote symmetry. To the extent that partners desire harmonious communication, to the extent that they prize reciprocity, asymmetry tends to interfere (cf. also Newcomb, 1953). Accordingly, we would expect that interpersonal closeness exerts forces toward symmetry. Conversely, asymmetry in involvement or commitment will, if sizeable and persistent, lead toward the disintegration of an adult social-emotional relationship.

Those are current impressions. Actually, there is little solid knowledge concerning the causes, effects, and limitations of interpersonal symmetry. Some sorts of sex-linked asymmetry are highly desirable—witness the French slogan, *Vive la différence.* Other forms of sex-role differentiation seem rightly deplored by contemporary liberationists. Yet the amount of symmetry in a closely involved pair is more than a question of personal value or caprice. It depends both on the function of the partners' relationship and on the social context in which they live.

The Pair in Its Social Context

In the close, stable community, still found in some parts of the world, there is little personal or interpersonal privacy. Activities and relationships occur in an atmosphere of almost total disclosure and surveillance. Social network and individual member are tightly interconnected. Urban society, in contrast, encourages anonymity and independence; it offers material abundance and individual privacy, but at the price of unraveling knots in the total social fabric. Whether urbanization represents "progress" is not here at issue; we merely consider its implications for the conduct of close relationships. The Person-Other dyad does not exist in isolation. How does its setting affect its interpersonal involvement, commitment, and symmetry?

Depth of Involvement Both the determinants and the effects of involvement are associated with the pair's social context. For example, recent work by sociologists and anthropologists (see Bott, 1971) has suggested that the tightness of external social networks varies inversely with the closeness of pair companionship. This observation appears to have wide generality, but there is controversy about why it occurs. We remain unclear how relatively important are connections between pair members and third parties, connections among the third parties themselves, the pressures the network places on the pair, the social and personal characteristics of network members, and so forth. If we were able to remove a pair entirely from all social anchorages, one might understand these mechanisms better, but we do not do this to human primates by other than multivariate statistical means.

No matter how deeply involving, though, no single relationship suffices to meet all of a person's needs. Some needs are better served by colleagues than by friends, and either of these are at times more satisfying than a spouse; a peer is occasionally less helpful than a superior or a subordinate (Weiss, 1968). Pair relationships, then, are not only challenged but also nourished by the partners' alternative involvements.

Dyadic involvement is largely a response to one's social context, but in turn it also affects the pair's interpersonal environment. The deeper a pair's emotional involvement, the less likely are the partners to have time or energy for intimate sharing with others. For that reason, membership in a commune or other living group may be threatened by deep dyadic involvements (Kanter, 1972; Slater, 1974). The nature of such cross-pressures, though, is today understood only vaguely.

Commitment as Affected by the Pair's Context   Many associations, most obviously the familial, are imposed on a person at birth. The development of relationships occurs in a restricted area of freedom. If external constraints are very great, as in the institution of arranged child marriage, they can possibly stunt the development of commitment to the other partner; yet the absence of all external structure or pressure would also seem to impair such commitment.

In the shifting social milieu experienced by many in the urbanized parts of our world, interpersonal commitments appear particularly important. Under some conditions they may seem confining, but they also serve to support the isolated individual. Associations may flourish either within the solid external boundaries indicated earlier in figure 2*a*, or within the internally reinforced intersection of figure 2*b*. The advantages and disadvantages of such alternatives can be important topics for systematic research.

Symmetry as Limited by Social Context   The authors of papers in this volume tend to empathize with contemporary affirmations of human equality. Today's male-female relations, in particular, are marked by efforts to find remedies for age-old patterns of imbalance. Our current social context exerts strong forces toward pair symmetry.

We must not deny, however, those basic forces that limit equality and promote differentiation or specialization. Power may be equalized in principle, but pair members do differ in their needs for dominance and in their ability to influence one another. And, while affection and communication are mutual matters, the performance of tasks encourages specialization. Maternal and paternal roles are hardly identical, no matter how egalitarian the spirit. And the more heterogeneous the backgrounds and opportunities of pair members, the more difficult is the achievement of balanced involvement.

In considering research priorities, we must eventually attend to the effects of social context on interpersonal relations. Yet, while blessed with case history and anecdotal material, we still lack systematic theory to guide empirical work.

Close Relationships: Disposable or Salvageable?

They [successful managers] can relate and disrelate themselves to others easily. . . . to be able to make these increasingly numerous on-off clicks in our interpersonal lives, we must be able to operate at a level of adaptability never before asked of human beings. [Toffler, 1970, pp. 117, 122]

A person with many achievements to his credit, but who has never achieved one real relationship-in-depth, cannot be sure that he has succeeded in life. But anyone who has achieved one relationship-in-depth, and has failed in many enterprises, can never be considered a failure. [Mace, 1969, p. 8]

Toffler's and Mace's words stand in polar opposition, though neither author would probably confine himself to an extreme view. Mace is aware of the problems inherent in overly deep relationships; Toffler confesses that there may be some optimum rate of relational breakups "that we exceed at our peril" (p. 122).

Despite my personal reservations about the single-minded pursuit of deep relationships, I do find unacceptable Toffler's image of tomorrow's modular people and their disposable interconnections. That image of the future seems based on assumptions of ever-accelerating mobility and affluence, of increasing material abundance and decreasing personal and interpersonal stability. Toffler's vision disturbs me for two reasons: I think his forecast is objectively incorrect, and I also believe its direction is subjectively undesirable.

An Alternative Forecast of Increasing Stability   Is it necessary that social change will continue at the pace of the past few decades? Shall all prediction follow linear extrapolation from recent trends? To the monolith of ever-upward-striving humanity can be counterposed the image of a repetitive natural cycle. Affluence may grow steadily; it may also decline. Mobility may grow; it can also stabilize. Freedom too may reach a peak and then suffer a reverse.

Recent economic events make it reasonable to forecast the peaking and decline of affluence. Limitations in energy resources make conceivable the reduction of geographic and social mobility. If communities change at a slower pace, the contexts of interpersonal relationships would again become more constraining and also more supporting.

Relationships as Valuable Containers   My image of relation*ship* also has value implications. If a "ship" is a vessel that contains interpersonal identities, then it carries important symbolic and emotional commodities. Where interpersonal involvement is high, it is important to preserve relationships. That idea differs from the view that relationships are disposable containers in a throwaway world.

At a time when containers are manufactured to be tossed out after they have served their immediate purpose, this image may seem old-fashioned. It is attuned, however, with the values of modern ecology—with the desire to preserve resources that exist in nature or are created by people. While it conflicts with the notion that modular people shall live forever in transit and at the call of the interpersonal marketplace, it is consistent with the belief that a healthy human society consists of relationships with long-term significance. This belief need not be rigid. It recognizes the pervasiveness of unsatisfying relationships, particularly in a heterogeneous society (see Russell, 1929); it endorses the efforts of people to build or rebuild alternative associations. But it also emphasizes the rightness and soundness of enduring close relationships.

Recapitulation

The reader may be distressed by the abstractness of my words, by the generality of my speculation. Let me therefore try to review.

I have focused on three fundamental aspects of close relationships: Involvement represents the degree of interpersonal closeness, commitment the extent of its intended continuity, and symmetry pertains to the quality of relationships. Conceived graphically, involvement is the size and shading of the intersection; commitment is the solidity of the pair's boundary, as held by the hull of its "ship" and influenced by the structure of its wider surrounding; symmetry refers to the relative size of the circles as well as their shading outside the intersection.

I am appalled by what remains unsaid, by the insufficiency of metaphor and analogy. I currently feel that we can merely grope toward the significance of intensive relationships in their wider context. If we know little about relationships that develop in childhood and youth, we know even less about those that remain or erode in old age.

Initially, I intended to construct paradoxes of interpersonal relationships, but my logic was inadequate. Perhaps this was because close relationships are the locus for ambivalence. Their very intensity complicates the recognition of positive and negative feelings; their very importance locks us into preconceived attitudes.

Some dilemmas of relationships can, however, be identified. Dilemmas of involvement and commitment pertain to the opposition between personal independence and interpersonal integration. Dilemmas of symmetry are affected by conflicts between the desire for achievement or specialization and that for harmonious communication. Much has been written about these dilemmas; I need not add more. It is likely, then, that research on close relationships will be conducted in an atmosphere of creative tension.

References

Bott, E. *Family and social network* (2nd ed.). London: Tavistock, 1971.

Bowlby, J. *Attachment and loss, I: Attachment.* New York: Basic Books, 1969.

Harlow, H. F. The nature of love. *American Psychologist,* 1958, *13*, 673–685.

Kanter, R. M. *Commitment and community.* Cambridge: Harvard University Press, 1972.

Levinger, G. Marital cohesiveness and dissolution: An integrative review. *Journal of Marriage and the Family,* 1965, *27*, 19–28.

Levinger, G. A three-level approach to attraction: Toward an understanding of pair relatedness. In T. L. Huston (Ed.), *Foundations of interpersonal attraction.* New York: Academic Press, 1974.

Levinger, G., & Snoek, J. D. *Attraction in relationship: A new look at interpersonal attraction.* Morristown, N.J.: General Learning Press, 1972.

Mace, D. R. *Marriage as vocation.* Philadelphia: Friends General Conference, 1969.

McCall, G. J., & Simmons, J. L. *Identities and interactions.* New York: Free Press, 1966.

Newcomb, T. M. An approach to the study of communicative acts. *Psychological Review,* 1953, *60*, 393–404.

Rubin, Z. *Liking and loving.* New York: Holt, Rinehart, & Winston, 1973.

Russell, B. *Marriage and morals.* New York: Liveright, 1929.

Simmel, G. In K. H. Wolff (Ed.), *The sociology of Georg Simmel.* New York: Free Press, 1950 (German version published in 1908).

Slater, P. *Earthwalk.* New York: Anchor Press/Doubleday, 1974.

Toffler, A. *Future shock.* New York: Random House, 1970.

Weiss, R. S. Materials for a theory of social relationships. In W. Bennis et al. (Eds.), *Interpersonal dynamics* (rev. ed.). Homewood, Ill.: Dorsey, 1968.

Weiss, R. S. *Loneliness: The experience of emotional and social isolation.* Cambridge, Mass.: M.I.T. Press, 1973.

2

Interpersonal Relationships: Some Questions and Observations

ELIZABETH DOUVAN

In efforts to map and define the province of social psychology, theorists have found it useful to distinguish conceptually among certain levels of social environmental variables. In this essay I differentiate three such levels: the interpersonal, the social organizational, and the cultural. Culture comprises technology and ideology, shared beliefs in (faith) and beliefs about (technology). Social organization is the role system. The interpersonal system comprises face-to-face interaction between whole persons. Both culture and social organization are normative systems; social organizational norms refer to relationships among persons. Culture encompasses these norms plus norms about relationships of persons to God and persons to nature. Social organization and the interpersonal both deal with interaction among persons, and the crucial distinction here consists of normativeness: social organization is a system of roles and the interpersonal is a system of relationships between and among whole persons. Interpersonal relationships are essentially nonnormative, the only exception being the norm of loyalty, in Parsons's terms the primitive precursor of solidarity.

Interpersonal relationships are face-to-face relationships between whole persons; they are affectively loaded, particularistic, and nonnormative. Role relations are partial, less affective, universalistic, and governed by norms, by shared expectations about the rights and obligations of role occupants.

To say that interpersonal relationships are nonnormative is not to say

In this paper I draw heavily on theoretical work done in collaboration with Martin Gold for a seminar on the Individual and the Social Environment and for a forthcoming book.

that they carry no expectations. People expect certain behaviors of those with whom they share interpersonal relationships, but only in the predictive sense. The expectations are not normative in the special moral sense implied by the term *norm*. When a friend behaves in an unpredicted way (except with disloyalty), we react not with moral indignation but with surprise and delight. The unexpected is in fact intrinsic to the concept of interpersonal relationships—a source of freshness and affect. The unexpected in role relationships, on the other hand, represents violation of shared moral expectations and occasions outrage, moral indignation, and sanctions. So long as a friend is loyal, he will not be the object of our indignation, and even vis-à-vis those moral prescriptions governing all people (e.g., laws) we will tend to wide tolerance of violations by a friend.

E. M. Forster once said that if he were ever faced with a choice between betraying a friend and betraying his nation-state, he would hope to have the courage to commit treason. I think Forster's profound insight into the nature of friendship was not unrelated to the issue of his clandestine, carefully hidden homosexuality.

Clearly, the interpersonal relationship is an ideal type which probably does not occur in reality. The closest approximation and prototype is the close friendship. Other close relationships like the parent-child relationship or the marital relationship are more heavily circumscribed by norms and are therefore farther along the continuum toward pure role relationships. The ideal type is close to Buber's "I-Thou." The existentialists focus on it, and most contemporary theories of therapy hold it out as an ideal—the nonmechanical, nonmanipulative contact between equals as whole persons.

We can raise many interesting issues and questions about close interpersonal relationships. For example, if we define them as nonnormative, where do interpersonal relationships derive their compelling force? It is a paradox that the relationship with greatest power to move people should be one that carries no demand for conformity to norms. Yet this seems to be the case, and we even have some evidence of it from empirical research. We know, for example, that overheard messages—those that apparently are not meant for us and can therefore carry no normative expectation of change—do indeed often influence attitudes. Sheila Zipf (1958) has demonstrated that overt attempts to influence a person give rise to resistance even when the person's previous feelings are consistent with the direction of influence.

In a study designed to test the effect of reward and punishment on performance of a sorting task, she found that when the experimenter explicitly and persistently urged subjects to speed up, resistance (measured by negative attitudes toward the experimenter and task) was greater, and performance less accurate, than when the experimenter simply stated the conditions for rewards and fines and did not indicate persistent interest in how subjects did. This was true even though subjects indicated a desire to perform well at the outset.

The very nonnormativeness that allows openness and nondefensiveness also allows openness to change. Empathy and taking the view of the other along with the retention of autonomy, the sense of freedom, seem to be at work here as conditions for influence and change.

Aligning the concept of interpersonal relationship with theories of power yields meaningful insights. For example, French and Raven (1959) in their theoretical classification distinguish the following four types and sources of power:

1. Coercive power—based on punishment and the threat of punishment

2. Legitimate power—based on evaluation in a situation where the evaluator and the person evaluated share a norm which holds that the evaluator has a legitimate right to influence

3. Referent power—power based on identification. "When an individual (P) is attracted to a person or group (O), he will achieve or maintain identification so long as he behaves, believes, or perceives as O does."

4. Expert power—based on the knowledge or skill of the individual holding influence

Both referent power and expert power seem applicable to the interpersonal realm. Often in friendships one detects clear evidence of identification: close friends often develop similar styles in voice and gesture, dress and manner. Young people often adopt the mannerisms of older distinguished colleagues with whom they share close ties. These influences are subtle and often unconscious, but they are palpable to the observer and represent very real influences of one partner on the other. A friend's knowledge and skill can represent both a resource in the relationship and a basis of attraction. Teachers who can allow non-role elements in their relationships with certain students can have extraordinary influence on these young people. An important element in the student's attraction to the teacher is often the teacher's broad knowledge. Wanting to "know as much" or "be as creative" as an admired teacher is certainly one of the critical thrusts in many of our early intellectual histories, just as is the feeling of wanting to be very good at something, to do very well, in response to an admired teacher's clear expectation that one can.

The other two power bases identified by French and Raven are alien to the interpersonal relationship. Evaluation and punitiveness are contradictory to it by definition, and the normative structure of legitimate power argues for the presence of a role relationship.

Open, nondefensive interaction is the keynote of interpersonal relationships. Nonthreateningness may be their unifying quality—the opportunity to behave freely, to explore potential aspects of the self, to achieve a new integration without risk of constant evaluation and sanction. Exchange is not the motive force in interpersonal relationships. Rather, it is pleasure in the relationship itself, meeting and accepting each other as whole persons, affirming each other's self.

In the process of clarifying and articulating the concept of interpersonal relationships, it has seemed a powerful concept for organizing and understanding large bodies of empirical findings in a productive way. We find its impact in areas where it was never intended or systematically noted. Rather like the child's early cognitive discoveries of sex or the theorist's invention of a new concept, having got hold of the concept, one finds that at least for a while it seems to explain all of reality.

So, for example, in the industrial literature, the Hawthorne effect appears to be the effect of growing interpersonalism in the work setting (reported in Homans, 1952). The women selected for the small experimental work group showed continually higher productivity even when the favored working conditions in their group were diminished. The women reported that it was easier for them to produce more in the small experimental group than it had been to produce at the normal rate in the regular factory. Two interpersonal aspects of the situation are especially noted by the experimenters as contributing to the effect. One was the development of a group life—the women talked, exchanged gifts for birthdays, and came to feel supportive and responsible for each other. The other aspect was the women's sense that management cared about them as people. Even when some of their privileges were withdrawn, they felt that the change was experimental and reflected an effort on management's part to determine optimum working conditions. They felt that they and their welfare were being considered. This can be seen as the introduction of interpersonalism into the employer-employee relationship.

Blauner's (1964) studies of automation lend themselves to similar interpretation. The assembly line—the most alienating system he studied—completely disallows even the rudiments of interpersonal interaction. The noise and speed alone are formidable obstacles to exchange. The mill workers he studied in southern factories, on the other hand, are friends or relatives before they enter the factory and can talk and sing together at the looms. The most highly automated system Blauner studied also supported the interpersonal life of workers. This was a large chemical plant which ran essentially on its own and required human labor only to check the machines periodically and to work as a team in emergencies. Between regular checking rounds the workers gathered in a small central room where they met and talked over a soup pot which was always simmering. Morale studies in industry can almost all be read in these terms rather than as demonstrations of the effect of participative decision making.

Hess and Shipman's (1965) research on the effects of different styles of parent-child interaction can be generalized as follows: the more interpersonal the relationship between mother and child, the greater the child's cognitive development will be.

In some cases the interpersonal relationship might have served as a powerful clarifying variable. In an ingenious use of a natural experimental situation, Siegel and Siegel (1957) studied the effect of membership and reference groups on college women's attitudes (F-scale scores). Two kinds of housing existed on the campus: sororitylike houses (called row houses) and dormitories. From earlier testing, it was known that dormitory residents scored lower on authoritarianism than row-house residents.

At the end of the first year, students were asked their housing preferences, and actual choice for sophomore year was arranged by lottery. Women who drew low lottery numbers got first choice. This gave the Siegels a pool of women whose preference (reference group) and actual living situation (membership group) was the row house, a pool where both choice and living arrangement was the dormitory, and a crucial third group who wanted the row house but got the dormitory. At the end of sophomore year the women again stated their preferences, and by that time some of the women in the third group shifted their choices from the row house to the dorm while others maintained their preference for the row house despite their year in a dorm. The women who continued to prefer the row house changed (toward decreased authoritarianism) less than those who had shifted preference to the dormitory.

The Siegels interpret this as the effect of the reference power of the group they preferred. But how was this effect transmitted? One possibility is that those girls who continued to prefer the row houses did so because their friends were in row houses. Interaction with these friends supported and maintained their authoritarian attitudes and their housing preference. The girls who had given up the preference by the end of sophomore year became committed to friendships in the dormitories, were influenced by these friendships (in the direction of lower authoritarianism scores, among other effects), and came to prefer the dorm. The power of the reference group was not large, and it seems possible that it might have been clearer if the Siegels could have partialed out the girls for whom the row house was merely an abstract prestige symbol from those for whom prestige and friendship both operated to support the girls' preexisting attitudes. Data about who were the girls' best friends and where they lived would have made this analysis possible.

The Requirements of Interpersonal Relationships

What does it take to form close interpersonal relationships; or, to put the question in a framework of individual differences, what kind of people are good at interpersonal relationships?

Trilling (1950) focuses on the essential requirement when he speaks of the struggle between love and power. To love is to open yourself to risk—the risk of rejection, hurt, unsettling surprise, and so forth. When you involve yourself closely with any other human system, you open your own system to forces over which you have no control. If you are preeminently concerned with predictability, security, certainty, control, and power, then clearly you should not involve yourself in *any* human relationship. Love exposes you to unpredictability, uncertainty, and to the risk of loss. Even if you love a saint you assume the ultimate risk of loss through death.

Involving oneself with others, then, implies at least a willingness to forgo some measure of security or power. And clearly one is willing because of the positive rewards of such involvement: rewards like self-affirmation, stimulation, variety, excitement. To make the choice one must prefer an open, exciting system to a closed, controlled and narrow one.

At a more concrete level, to be good at close interpersonal relationships requires many of the same qualities that are required for any creative enterprise. Besides a pleasure in risk taking, you need a measure of narcissism—an appreciation for this self that is to be disclosed and affirmed in interpersonal relationships, a self-awareness and a taste for life that are both intimately related to narcissism (cf. Erikson, 1950, on trust in self and trust in the world). You need a certain level of energy and liveliness that may spring from narcissism but takes the form of—is organized into—personal expressiveness. You need a playful tolerance—a capacity to suspend judgment—in order to be engaged by and engaging to other people, and an *investment* in surprise, a pleasure in the unexpected.

But interpersonal creativity has some special requirements that other forms of creativity do not demand. One of these is the ability to express dependency. All creativity probably requires an element of passivity—you have to be able to dream, to make contact with the unconscious or the infantile or primary process or whatever label we give that inner spring, and to do so requires a certain passivity or ability to dissociate from imposing, compelling externals at least fleetingly. But the gift for intimacy requires a more specific form of passivity—the willingness to hand over control by depending on another, however briefly.

And I think this is extremely hard for people to do. In Haley's (1963) terms, depending on another always means placing oneself in a "one-down" position. Let me give some examples. It is hard for people to ask favors of other people. The hardest part of any political campaign is getting people to make finance calls—no one likes to ask other people for money. I think that a measure of the extent to which community exists in a neighborhood can be devised simply through recording the extent and mutual patterning of borrowing among its members. A personal example (which is therefore available for refined phenomenological analysis) has to do with child-care arrangements. At the beginning of a semester ten years ago, I found myself suddenly with a collapse in my child-care arrangements and a teaching schedule that required me to be away from home three afternoons a week. Close to panic, I turned to a relatively new neighbor who had a child at home the same age as my daughter. I asked if she could take care of my preschooler those three afternoons, which she did in exactly the same spirit I would have—to be helpful and a good neighbor and also because any mother of a three-year-old knows that two little ones are much easier and more pleasant to take care of and entertain than one alone.

I have thought about this encounter many times. It was hard for me to ask a substantial favor from this neighbor whom I knew only moderately well. It had not occurred to me to use the neighbor as a baby-sitter until I was forced to do so by circumstance. My sitter arrangement of choice was a formal contractual one. I had hired a young woman. It has since occurred to me how much we would all have lost if my contract had not collapsed. I would never have had the amazement and joy of so generous and graciously presented a gift. She would not have had the opportunity to give the gift of her neighborly and human concern. We might never have become such close sisters or so close that people have asked if we were sisters. The reserve and distance between us diminished significantly in the train of this exposure of dependency and support.

What does it imply that we so often avoid dependency and choose the contract route first? Most of us, I think, would do what my friend did—that is, respond to another human being in need. It fits our internal picture of ourselves as humane and generous people, and it is self-affirming in this core feature. Yet we often imply by our apparent preference for contract that we do *not* assume that most people include such qualities in their core definitions of self. Or perhaps we are so afraid of exposing our dependency that we would deny other people the opportunity to affirm themselves in important core elements with grand gestures. In discussing this incident with students I have been impressed with the following conclusion, among many: the failure of community in our society is not a failure in willingness to give so much as a fear of asking, of allowing the exposure of dependency. So many students have told me that they were taught (and usually by fathers) to give generously any support they could but to depend on no one. Only very secure upper-class students—mostly Quakers—and certain of those who have learned through extraordinary vulnerability how supportive real friends can be (and here I would place Forster)—break the mold of isolated independence that dominates our modern myth and model of social interaction.

Heaven knows the alternative—choosing the unencumbering simplicity of contractual arrangements—has its appeal in situations like the political campaign. After nagging some grandiose volunteers for a while, it looks like a beautiful ploy to be able to say, as one can in contract, "Go to hell, I'll take my business elsewhere," and to march off with our five thousand dollars.

Another example—again from my child-care arranging (which might lead us to conclude with certain analytic writers that women will do in the interests of their children many things they will not do for themselves; I tend rather to see child raising as simply another opportunity for a woman to grow and learn new skills because it presents new challenges). For quite a few years, when our children were small, we had living with us young Norwegian women who acted as all-around helpers. They were lovely people and always became very much a part of our family. They are all still good friends.

The reaction of many of my acquaintances to this arrangement fascinated me, partly because I could not imagine having this reaction myself: it was a sense of invasion. The question I was asked over and over again was, "Don't you find it a terrible invasion of privacy to have someone else in your home?" Now these attractive young women were by no means wallflowers. We live in a university community and when the evening work was finished, if they were not crucially needed, they were off having a good time. My questioners knew this; yet, apparently the presence of a helper during the daytime when I was at home seemed to them to limit my privacy. What I could never understand was how in the world a mother of preschool children could find any privacy to defend in the first place. My response—of course, entirely rational—was that what was crucial with preschoolers were extra hands, not an illusion of privacy.

Some young women today are discovering and acting on the same set of insights that I developed then, yet many women I meet even now say that they cannot imagine managing another relationship while raising their children. The model seems to be one of limited resources which will be depleted, rather than the equally tenable conception that the addition of another adult will add to and free up resources previously unavailable. It was often expressed directly as a fear of involvement and dependency—in this case the possibility of someone else's dependency, someone else for whom one might somehow be responsible.

What is this fear of involvement and dependency? Where does it come from, and why does it seem to grow and flourish like a noxious weed in our particular world? We could devote a whole volume to this question—spinning out the elements in our immigrant and frontier heritage, in primitive Kleinian mechanisms, in industrialism and alienation, geographic mobility and the breakdown of extended kinship or of communal ties, in the nature of our child-raising ideology and technique—the elements in all these areas that have contributed to both the illusion of omnipotent autonomy and the unwillingness to admit interdependence. It would be a volume well spent and filled with piquant paradox.

I would like to add one other requirement of interpersonal creativity—again, a requirement that is unique to this area of performance. It is the ability to bear, accept, absorb, and resolve interpersonal conflict and hostility. In my marginal contact with the encounter movement—through the stories I hear and the papers students submit—I had long ago come to the conclusion that, for all the lip service given to love in the movement, the underlying criterion most often used to assess the success of a group had, in practice, nothing to do with love but rather had specifically to do with how much and how openly hostility was expressed. Finally, lo and behold, a group of theorists came along who said so in plain language and offered to train people in how to have fights with each other. My response to these theorists—and to the fact that they draw large groups of customers—is that those people who must be trained to fight have obviously not grown up in large Irish families.

I suppose it is true—though intuitively I reject the thought—that there are in the world many people who do not know how or cannot bear to fight. But then, of course, they will have a very hard time forming or maintaining intense personal relationships. No two human beings are identical. If two people become intimate, they must expose and clarify areas of difference between them. They can either choose to bear and to tolerate the differences, as they would with strangers, or they can with youthful verve and all good will set out to change each other (read "fight") over the course of twenty-five or fifty years and *then* settle for tolerating the differences that simply will not yield to the treatment. One way or the other, intimacy and conflict will have a common fate. We found evidence of this in developmental analysis of children's concepts of friendship (Douvan & Adelson, 1966, pp. 220–228). As they grew in understanding of friendship, girls came to see the relationship as resilient enough and important enough to absorb and resolve conflict.

In recognizing this tie between intimacy and hostility, the encounter movement has achieved an insight—although I have reservations about the direction of its application in the movement. I recognize that hostility is often used in interpersonal relationships as a last-ditch effort to salvage waning intimacy. One need only think back to friendships that cooled or infatuations that diminished or to parent-adolescent exchange in which the abandoned partner attacked in an effort to regain intimacy. People who are deeply committed feel that *any* intimacy is better than none and recognize intuitively that when all else fails, attack is likely to engage the deeply personal. But these are relationships with both history and equity—at least for one partner. I do not think that a ritual rerun of the external features of intimacy in a group with no history or investment is the same as real intimacy.

Sources of Interpersonal Isolation

Let me shift now to the topic of our contemporary world and to some of the forces that seem to push us toward greater and greater systematization and rationalization of relationships, toward isolation and loneliness.

Two crucial elements in contemporary ideology seem to underlie fear of personal involvement and incapacity for commitment. These are our exaggerated interpretation of the Romantic dilemma, the conflict we see between the person as individual and the person as social; and the apparently increasing belief that there is such a thing as a free lunch.

Americans have carried the ideas of individualism and unencumbered autonomy about as far as they can go. As a people we are peculiarly uncomfortable with the idea of social connectedness, and tend to see the force of society as a corruption of innocence, a dangerous consuming force that can destroy the individual, his personhood, and his freedom. The tension between civilization—Europe and the eastern seats of culture—on the one hand, and the lure of the West—that symbol of unfettered and untamed masculinity—on the other, is still palpable in its effects on our consciousness. Witness the fear and hatred of the eastern establishment, the "they" of paranoid preoccupations in the White House transcripts exposed during the Watergate hearings. We can, it seems to me, hardly imagine its power on those waves of immigrants who carried the guilty knowledge that they had abandoned their parents and European homelands. For them the choice must have demanded an enormous mobilization of aggressive energy—to break from the past, reject earliest ties, abandon loved ones sometimes to a fate of misery and starvation, and then to defend against the guilt and anxiety that such behavior normally implies. Immigration must in many cases have been an act of transcending selfishness and narcissism—a preeminently adolescent act—exactly the act we expect and survival demands of every adolescent at a symbolic level, when the adolescent psychologically escapes from his family to continue the life of his own generation.

But symbolic acts are different from acting out, partly in that they have different consequences. For men literally to abandon the family means that they must also abandon the past. Any element of that past carries the implicit danger of rearousing overwhelming guilt and anxiety that could destroy personhood. The men of the frontier had to keep moving; they literally ran for their lives. Ties and roots, the trappings of civilization, could destroy them. Once having made the choice for isolated autonomy, they often made it again in the new world. Wives and children were often deserted by men who headed west. Sennett's (1970) middle-class families in nineteenth-century Chicago still showed a high rate of dissolution through desertion by male heads. Mumford (1965) says that the European immigrants brought with them an eighteenth-century European preoccupation with the innocent, primitive, and exotic—and they took up their search for it in the West. The dichotomy between man and society took on in action the clarity and decisiveness of Rousseauian theory.

The choice became either social relatedness or authentic selfhood. American males withdrew from self-exposure and dependency, and in time, as Erikson (1950) has so compellingly outlined, Americans developed a system of "scientific" child raising that would raise the emotionally retentive young men whom the system needed to keep it moving. Fear of encumbrance assumed prominence in our national myth and consciousness.

The isolated narcissistic conception of individualism, a concept of the individual separate from and in opposition to socialization, laid the groundwork for the second element of the national myth that I want to consider. A regnant sense of individual need and desire—as distinguished from the needs of the group—combined with affluence to produce the free-lunch theory, namely, the assumption that choices do not carry costs, that acts have no consequences, that resources are unlimited, and that using them does not change them. Even the early statements of the ecology movement were shot through with such assumptions. While it was important to warn against wanton pollution and destruction of resources, early statements sounded as though pollution were a recent invention, one that could be eliminated with good will and concerted effort. Rarely did one find explicit recognition that all organic processes involve the production of waste. Except for small and later voices, the emphasis was less on conservation and husbandry than on finding a "solution" for the problem.

This same idea—of unlimited progress and unlimited resources—shaped our ideas of social life. We denied death and aging and developed into a youth-centered culture in which middle-aged people behaved as though they *could* go home again, start over again, make a new life, and deny the past. But such a view makes for very little commitment. When things became too touchy or too painful for those nineteenth-century middle-class husbands and fathers in Chicago, they simply disappeared and moved on; they denied the past and started over.

The victims of this disregard for commitment—the wives and children, the exploited and put down—did the best they could, usually not very well. Later, when victims began to assert *their* rights to individuality, their assertion often took a form fashioned from the father-husband's model. Elkins (1959) has pointed to a critical generalization in his analysis of the institution of slavery: that the social conditions directing the form of slavery also shaped the form that abolition would take. In other words, the same social forces that lead to a problem will also condition the dimension and the form of its solution.

Early in the women's movement (and even now, upon discovering Betty Friedan), women frequently reacted with, "Why should I subjugate my needs to those of other people?" They then proceeded to leave home, husband, and children to realize their own "unique potential." They behaved very much like American frontier males, nineteenth-century Chicago husbands, perhaps their own fathers. The rate of runaway wives has increased dramatically in recent years.

Of course we all have fantasies of walking out. I have walked out in my mind hundreds of times—and probably you have, too. With me, the problem is always that in my mind I get as far as the front door, and then have no idea where to go. Fantasy and acting out one's fantasy are different and have different effects.

Why should people not walk away from their troubles? Mainly because walking away does not change them; and walking away does not undo all of the choices implied by a home and family and collection of troubles. You do not wipe out the past by turning away from it; you do not expunge the consequences and costs of choices by moving on. The choice to have children makes you a parent—there is no way to become an unparent, or to both be and not be a parent. There is no such thing as a free lunch.

Another paradox in the relation of victim and victimizer: a focus of resentment against the white male establishment in both the Black movement and the women's movement rests on the manipulative and inhuman way in which dominant white males have related to people—as "objects" to be manipulated in the service of self-centered needs. Certainly many WASP males in power positions are insensitive and unexpressive, and they have developed an institutional structure that stresses nonhuman values. The values of upper-class schools for boys encourage norms of universalism and values of an "impersonal" style of behavior (McArthur, 1955). The response of the victims—because of their history of manipulation and exploitation—is to fear any relationship with members of the dominant group that is not carefully circumscribed by role obligations and contract. Personalism in this context has too often been just another form of manipulation. But here again we have an example of an oppressed group adopting a form— contract and distance—originally developed by the oppressor.

Current Trends in Interpersonal Relationships

Some recent changes in our culture offer hope of critical shifts in our values and capabilities in the interpersonal realm. While I do not see the encounter movement as the answer to our alienation, its popularity is a hopeful sign in that it suggests that Americans are dissatisfied with the depth of their human contacts.

The most hopeful single thing I see happening is the reassertion by young women and men of their right to be fully human, particularly the right of males to be in touch with their feelings and to take the full prerogatives of parenthood—asserting the legitimacy of sharing in the joy as well as in the grubby work of rearing little children. This movement holds real promise, I think, of undoing some of the terrible denial and constriction that the heritage of immigration and the frontier imposed on previous generations of American males. I am impressed with the compassion many of these new-style young fathers feel for their own fathers for the losses that life forced on them. The young men are rejecting the model of their fathers' generation, but they are not rejecting their fathers as persons.

The political scene—in which I am an amateur but have a long family history of professionals—offers other hopeful paradigms for study. Irish politicians in particular, but old ward politicians in general, are people for whom the interpersonal rather than power itself is the golden ring of the game. Personal power through attraction and commitment is part of their reward, but their reward also includes humor, delight in the human contact, aesthetic appreciation for the ragtag and bobtail that we call the human condition. They extend themselves, ingratiate themselves with charm and humor, because people engage them and they want to be loved. As I watched Haldeman, Erlichman, and Mitchell, I kept thinking that Irish Democrats could not have done what these men did—certainly not in the same style. The self-certainty (and arrogance) of these men who thought that their judgment about other people's welfare was superior or infallible, could not, I think, have developed in people whose basic article of faith is that we are all sinners together. In any Irish gathering, humor would be quickly used to tame such pomposity. Closeness to the folk is both a characteristic of Irish culture and an aspiration for many Irish (and other old-style) politicians.

In an analysis of data from a study of delegates to the 1972 national political conventions, we found one group of male delegates with a curious mix of political styles. They were party loyalists for whom the party as an organization was critical: they thought, for example, that creating a winning slate was the preeminent goal of the convention, more important than platform positions or social issues. In this respect they were highly professional; institutional party loyalty marked their political orientation. At the same time, they showed what we designated an "auxiliary" style to a degree unmatched by any other group of male delegates. This label suggests the elements of their style, and also that we expected it to be a style more common among women than among men. These same professional "old pols" said that initially they had become involved in politics because of a friend or relative who was active or was running for office. When asked what they liked best about political activity and the convention, they referred to interpersonal gratifications and they alluded to their own interpersonal skills as the qualities that made them successful in politics.

These hybrid professionals—who mixed professionalism and personalism—were locally rooted, middle-aged, middle-level party workers from smaller cities. They were not at the center of national power, nor were they as economically successful as the men in the national power elite. Apparently they were in the political game at least in part for the pleasure of its human contact. I think we would do well to study this group further to learn the sources and effects of their social motivation and skill.

References

Blauner, R. *Alienation and freedom: The factory worker and his industry.* Chicago: University of Chicago Press, 1964.

Douvan, E., & Adelson, J. *The adolescent experience,* chap. 6, pp. 174–228. New York: Wiley, 1966.

Elkins, S. *Slavery: A problem in American institutional and intellectual life.* Chicago: University of Chicago Press, 1959.

Erikson, E. H. *Childhood and society.* New York: Norton, 1950.

French, J. R. P., & Raven, B. The bases of social power. In D. Cartwright (Ed.), *Studies in social power.* Ann Arbor, Mich.: Institute for Social Research, 1959.

Friedan, B. *The feminine mystique.* New York: Dell, 1963.

Haley, J. *Strategies of psychotherapy.* New York: Grune & Stratton, 1963.

Hess, R. D., & Shipman, Y. C. Early experience and the socialization of cognitive modes in children. *Child Development,* 1965, *36,* 869–886.

Homans, G. C. Group factors in worker productivity. In Swanson, G. E., Newcomb, T. M., & Hartley, E. E. (Eds.) *Readings in Social Psychology,* pp. 637–649. New York: Holt, 1952.

McArthur, D. C. Personality differences between middle and upper classes. *Journal of Abnormal Social Psychology,* 1955, *50,* 247–254.

Mumford, L. The American in Europe. In *The human prospect,* pp. 191–201. Carbondale: Southern Illinois University Press, 1965.

Sennett, R. *Families against the city: Middle class homes of industrial Chicago, 1872–1890.* Cambridge: Harvard University Press, 1970.

Siegel, A. E., & Siegel, S. Reference groups, membership groups, and attitude change. *Journal of Abnormal and Social Psychology,* 1957, *55,* 360–364.

Trilling, L. I. *The liberal imagination: Essays on literature and society.* New York: Viking Press, 1950.

Zipf, S. G. An experimental study of resistance to influence. Ph.D. dissertation, University of Michigan, 1958.

3

Private Lives and Public Order: A Critical View of the History of Intimate Relations in the United States

HOWARD GADLIN

Prefatory Note

This chapter attempts an interpretation of some of the changes in intimate relationships over the past 300 years of American history. Clearly the scope of the essay must be limited. I have chosen to concentrate on close personal relationships between opposite-sex adults. Furthermore, since there are striking class differences in the form and content of intimacy, I shall limit myself to a discussion of middle-class relationships. This focus reflects the greater availability of relevant materials for this class.

One word on definition: I have avoided a definition of intimacy because the essay is about the changes in the social meaning of interpersonal closeness. Our vocabulary often changes more slowly than do behaviors, attitudes, values, and consciousness. Consequently we find that many of the same words that colonial Americans used to describe facets of intimacy are still in use today. Increasingly, I am convinced that these words—words such as *love, affection, closeness, caring,* and so on— have significantly changed meaning over the years. My analysis will suggest some ways in which these changes are related to other developments in American social history.

Also, a comment on method: Even with someone one knows well, it is difficult to understand the world as the other experiences it. Clearly, it

As will be apparent, I have borrowed freely from the work of many scholars. They are not, of course, responsible for my interpretations of their work. I am particularly indebted to Steve Nissenbaum who inspired much of my interest in these problems and who has influenced my thinking more than can ever be surmised by the frequency with which I cite his work.

is much more difficult to grasp the psychological experiences of people from past epochs. Pertinent information is limited and often sketchy. At most times I will be interpreting the interpretations of other historians. Yet I must attempt to project myself into the past, and toward that end this essay is intentionally speculative. For stylistic purposes, I shall not flag each bit of speculation. Similarly, although I recognize that the analysis presented here homogenizes what must have been a diversity of experiences, I will speak monomorphically of intimacy in various periods. The pictures drawn are composites. There is no single description of middle-class intimacy for a particular historical epoch. The experience of intimacy varied as a function of numerous variables: ethnic and religious background, geographical region, local economic and social conditions, and so on. I have attempted to identify some of the more salient features, selecting in particular (1) those that seem to appear repeatedly, and (2) those that have some bearing on our understanding of the present. Again it is primarily for purposes of stylistic clarity that I shall avoid many qualifications that the following typifications require.

The thesis to be argued in this essay is that intimate relationships, as we understand them today, emerged during the early decades of the nineteenth century. Those years mark a rapidly accelerating pace of modernization in America. The transformation of intimate relationships can best be understood within the context provided by the rapid urbanization and industrial development that characterize that period. It is the epoch in which the world of work is severed from the world of the home. For the individual, this separation of the public from the private leads to a great expansion of personal consciousness. Contemporary forms of interpersonal intimacy emerge with this self-conscious bourgeois individual whose life is torn between the separated worlds of work and home. Individualism and intimacy are the Siamese twins of modernization.

To illustrate this interpretation of the changing nature of intimacy, four historical epochs will be examined: the colonial (mid-1600s), the Jacksonian (1825–40), the second decade of the twentieth century, and the contemporary period (post-1940). These periods appear to indicate significant stages in the metamorphosis of the United States from traditional to modern society. Reinhard Bendix (1968) has attempted to differentiate between modern and traditional society without either romanticizing the past or glorifying the present. I shall employ his conceptualization of the differences in this analysis:

> Typically, traditional societies achieve intense solidarity in relatively small groups that tend to be isolated from one another . . . and that also tend to create for their individual participants an intensity of emotional attachment and rejection which modern men find hard to appreciate and which they would probably find personally intolerable. Typically, modern societies achieve little solidarity in relatively small groups . . . these groups tend to be highly interdependent at an impersonal level. In this setting individual participants experience an intensity of emotional attachment and rejection at two levels which hardly exist in traditional society, namely in the nuclear family at its best and worst, and at the national level. [P. 320]

The implications of this distinction can best be concretized by turning directly to an examination of intimate relationships in the colonial era.

Formal Intimacy: The Colonial Experience

Among the most striking characteristics of the colonial era was the fact that personal life was not private, nor was it separated from public institutions. The household fell under the authority of the community; it was directed under the guidance and surveillance of the community to serve a multiplicity of functions. The colonial household was a business, a school, a vocational institute, a church, a house of correction, and a welfare institution (Demos, 1970). What we call interpersonal relations took place within the boundaries of the performance of these functions, not separated from them. Intervention in malfunctioning families was expected and generally accepted. For example, a child might be placed in another home if the authorities deemed he or she was not receiving a proper upbringing (Rothman, 1971). Similarly, if a married man or woman ran off with someone else, he or she would be punished and placed back within his or her 'rightful' home. Even within one's own household, surveillance was the norm.

Indeed, in the colonial era, intimacy primarily connotes physical proximity, and in that sense intimacy was an inevitable consequence of the architecture of daily life. Within households, people were almost always within monitoring range of one another. Families were large and houses small; of the few rooms there were, most were multipurpose. Even if a person were alone in a room, almost any of his activities could be overheard, since plaster walls were virtually nonexistent (Demos, 1970). Furthermore, within a room private space was minimized since beds were typically shared and benches more common than single chairs. Many people seem to have engaged in illicit sex in a bed occupied by more than the lovers, as court testimony shows. Court records also indicate that even for those who were married sexual life was rarely private. Clearly, privacy was rarely possible indoors, and it makes little sense to speak of "personal" life in such a context (Flaherty, 1967). Still, there is more to intimacy than mere proximity, and it is necessary to inquire of the shared affections, sexual passions, and other indicators of closeness that differentiate intimate from more impersonal relationships. Certainly, as Edmund Morgan (1966) observed, colonial men and women formed "deep and warm attachments," and the content and meaning of those attachments can be examined.

In our experience, informality is a primary indicator and accompaniment of intimacy. Impersonal relations tend to be formal, and personal relationships informal. In the colonial era, although there was a range of intimacy, there seems to have been much less difference between personal and impersonal relations than there is currently. Indeed, within a colonial community, it is barely meaningful to speak of impersonal relations. At the same time, it is clear that even the closest of relationships was formal to a degree we would today find not only awkward but contradictory to intimacy. This formality between people whose lives are so completely intertwined could be seen as one means of preserving some distance in the face of an overbearing intimacy. It is more likely that the formality accurately reflects the degree to which even the most intimate relationships were embedded within the formal social order. It must be noted that whatever personal attachment existed between man and woman in colonial society existed within a context of severe paternal authoritarianism, a basic misogyny, and a fundamentalist Christian distrust of uncontrolled earthly pleasures and human passion. In such a context love was not the basis for a relationship but the result of it. For the Puritan it was a duty and obligation to love one's spouse (Morgan, 1966). In fact, failure to love one's spouse was itself a kind of disobedience to God. This notion continued well into the eighteenth century as, for example, in *The Well-Ordered Family* where Benjamin Wadsworth could exclaim:

The Great God commands thee to love her. . . . This duty of love is mutual, it should be performed by each, to each of them. They should endeavor to have their affections really, cordially and closely knit, to each other. . . . The indisputable authority, the plain command of the Great God, required Husband and Wives, to have and manifest very great affection, love and kindness to one another. They should (out of Conscience to God) study and strive to render each other's life easy, quiet, and comfortable; to please, gratifie and oblige one another, as far as lawfully they can. [Cited in Morgan, 1966, pp. 47–48]

Two features of this passage, representative of numerous others like it in tone and content, are noteworthy. First, it reveals a profound fear of the absence of affection in the family. Such preachments are unnecessary when affection and kindness are generated naturally within the dynamic of modal relationships of a culture. These writings remind one of the appeals for brotherhood and against "prejudice" that were popular in recent years, as the issues of racism and discrimination surfaced. Such appeals are of course understandable in the face of an important social problem, but as historical indicators they point to the lack of that for which they ask.

The family was the core institution for all aspects of colonial life. Peace and harmony within union of man and woman were essential not just to family but to general social stability as well. Many writers have pointed to an almost obsessive concern in the colonial era with maintaining peace, especially domestic peace. The writings of church leaders abound with proscriptions against physical and verbal abuse between husband and wife. The court records of colonial villages are replete with instances of complaints like the following, of which John Dunham was convicted in Plymouth, "abusive carriage toward his wife in continual tiranising over her, and in pticulare for his late and abusive and uncivill carryage in endeavoring to beate her in a deboist manor" (Demos, 1970, p. 93); or that of Joan Miller charged for "beating and reviling her husband, and egging her children to healp her, bidding them knock him in the head, and wishing his victuals might coak him" (Demos, 1970, p. 93). And it should be noted that it was for crimes of aggression, not for sexual transgressions, that the Puritans reserved their most severe punishments. It seems reasonable to suppose that the physical intimacy of colonial life must have created fairly explosive situations, particularly within households. If so, then love and affection would have been seen as important, not as ends in themselves, but as a force to counteract that explosiveness.

That love and affection were not sought for their own sake, nor were they the basis of relations, is clear when we pursue the second significant feature of Wadsworth's prescription for a Well-Ordered Family— feeling and emotion are understood as basically antisocial. As such they require "governance" by placement within boundaries drawn by reason and shaped by the will. As Morgan has so nicely demonstrated, even in matters of love, affections were commanded, although often unsuc- cessfully, to act according to the choices of reason (Morgan, 1966). It is within such a conceptual framework that it made sense to speak of an obligation to love or of "endeavoring to have affections closely knit." Often in colonial writings, when passions are discussed it is within a consideration of manipulating and directing them.

Along these lines we can observe that it was not on the basis of having established a promising relationship that one decided to marry, but on the basis of being ready to marry that one went out to find a mate. Few young single people lived alone in colonial America (Morgan, 1966; Demos, 1970; Flaherty, 1967). Being ready to marry meant being ready to assume financial independence and full social responsibility within the community. Typically this occurred when a man obtained property. People did not often marry before they were economically independent, and once independent they were expected to marry. Marrying, in such a culture, meant selecting a suitable mate. "Suitable" meant of similar standing in the community and with full familial approval. Ideally then, even in the search for a marriage partner, reason not passion was expected to dominate. Morgan (1966, p. 53) cites a letter proposing marriage in which the suitor emphasizes his ten reasons for believing the union would be a good one, that his decision is a rational one:

> 21y   That upon serious, earnest and frequent seeking of God . . . my thought have still been determined and fixed upon yourself as the most suitable Person for me.
> 31y   In that I have not been led hereunto by fancy (as too many are in like cases) but by sound Reason and judgment.

But with all the emphasis on directing passion and feeling within the bounds of reason, I do not believe that people in colonial society actually believed they could alter the *nature* of basic feelings or impulses. As famous as the Puritans were for their restrictions of sexuality, their efforts went primarily toward the control of behavior rather than the manipulation and shaping of impulse. The colonial attitude toward the impulses they sought to curb through restrictions on behavior was highly ambivalent. On the one hand, man's basic nature was seen as depraved. On the other hand, that depravity was accepted as natural (Rugoff, 1971). Within that framework, sexual feelings were acknowledged as natural, and even sexual pleasure could be accepted as good, within limits. The limits were clear; sexual behavior was sanctioned only within marriage. Even within marriage people had to take care that sexual pleasure did not distract them from religious and social obligation. It was because people were basically sexual that their sexuality had to be restricted. It had to be restricted to ensure the cohesion and proper functioning of society (Morgan, 1966; Demos, 1970). The family was the core of society and marriage the coming together of two families. Sexuality was acceptable within the bounds of marriage. Fornication and adultery were crimes because they represented the union of two people outside of marriage—that is, in colonial terms, outside of society. Sexual intimacy outside of marriage was antisocial and necessitated punishment. The more antisocial the behavior, the stronger the punishment. Thus sodomy, which was seen as beyond the limits of sociality, was punishable by death. So too was adultery, at least in principle; Morgan, however, reports only three recorded executions for adultery. At any rate, multiple offenses brought more severe punishment. But it is not the mere fact of punishment of sexuality outside of marriage that reveals the colonials' fear of the antisocial aspect of sexuality. The form of punishment, too, demonstrates that sexuality was a public not a personal matter. Our culture removes criminals from society; colonial Americans placed offenders on display (Rothman, 1971). Punishment, no matter how severe, no matter how horrendous the crime, was always a public matter, an occasion for the gathering of the community. Indeed, Demos (1970) has suggested that for people so accustomed to, even dependent upon, surveillance, shame must be a central component to the processes by which their behavior is controlled. Certainly the punishments themselves—whippings, the stocks, public fines and executions, often accompanied by moral preachments—suggest that shame played a central role.

Whatever the processes by which such punishments functioned, the public nature of the punishment is itself a sort of acknowledgment of the impulses. Certainly there was no pretending that sexual feelings did not exist. And indeed, when sexuality occurred within marriage, sexual pleasure was accepted as a very important part of sexual intercourse. "Felicity" was a common euphemism for sexual pleasure, and it was treated as any other earthly delight, acceptable as long as it was kept within the bounds of social responsibility and order (Nissenbaum, 1966).

If social rationality provided the psychological boundaries of emotionality, paternal authority represented that rationality institutionalized. Although colonial women, unlike many of their European counterparts, had some clearly defined legal rights, there was no doubt that women were men's inferiors. In fact, they were their subjects. The primary metaphor used to discuss marriage and the family was governance, and it was the man who was the head of the family. As such he represented the authority of both the social order and God, and his wife was unambiguously under his dominion. For the woman, her legal status as subject was reduplicated in the expectations of her role. This is amply demonstrated by statements such as the following justification of the principles of paternal authority offered by a Pilgrim pastor: "since differences will arise and be seen, and so the one must give way, and apply unto the other; this, God and nature layeth upon the woman, rather than upon the man" (Demos, 1970). "A reverend subjection" was how the pastor chose to describe the appropriate attitude of a woman to her man (Demos, 1970). Willard's *Compleat Body of Divinity* was less subtle. Since the husband was "the Conduit Pipe of the variety of blessings that God suplyeth them with," it was expected that her reverence would be a combination of love and fear. This was not to be "a *slavish Fear* which is nourished with hatred or aversion; but a *noble* and *generous Fear,* which proceeds from Love" (Morgan, 1966; p. 45). Clearly, in colonial America heterosexual intimacy, at least in marriage, was inextricably fused with domination. Social stability, in turn, was built around this domination.

In a society with a clear hierarchical organization, social status serves as a mold within which the contents of intimacy are shaped. Social status therefore provides limits to the meaning of intimacy, assuring that all relations reproduce authority relations. In such a manner the equalizing potentiality of caring can be contained. Thus, when men and women have different status in society, their personal relations have different meanings to each. In colonial America, any extramarital sexual relation on the part of a woman was considered adulterous. For the man only sexual relations with a woman who was married or betrothed was adultery. Demos has noted the significance of this difference. Whereas a wife's adultery was both a violation of her marriage and an offense against community, a husband's adultery was only a violation of his marriage (Demos, 1970).

There is, in addition, ample evidence that there was a strong misogyny associated with the unequal status of men and women. Many ministers found it necessary to speak out against the opinion that women were at best a "necessary evil." John Cotton defended women against such notions by asserting:

> Women are Creatures without which there is no comfortable living for man: it is true of them what is wont to be said of Governments, *That bad ones are better than none:* They are a sort of Blasphemers then who dispise and decry them, and call them *a necessary Evil,* for they are *a necessary Good;* such as it was not good that man should be without. [Morgan, 1966, p. 29]

One has to wonder about the quality of love and the content of affectionate bonds in such a culture. We like to think of love as relatively free of conditions. It is clear, however, that in colonial America love was conditional upon its recipient remaining within the boundaries of social expectations. When caring went beyond those limits, people were anything but sympathetic. For example, when the wife of the Connecticut governor went mad, allegedly from attending too seriously to intellectual matters, it was observed:

> Her husband, being very loving and tender of her was loath to grieve her, but he saw his error, when it was too late. For if she had attended her household affairs, and such things as belong to women, and not gone out of her way and calling to meddle in such things as are proper for men whose minds are stronger etc. she had kept her wits, and might have improved them usefully and honorably in the place God had set her. [Morgan, 1966, p. 42]

At times it seems as if women were liked for being the emotional, irrational creatures they were despised for being. Indeed, well into the latter half of the eighteenth century when the Puritan influence had waned, when some women such as Mary Wollstonecraft had begun to defy social convention by obtaining education and openly advocating women's rights, even the more enlightened men, such as Benjamin Rush and Ben Franklin, argued for the education of women not as a means to obtaining greater social equality but as a method of controlling their excessive emotionality. Rush, the father of American psychiatry, argued "that the female temper can only be governed by reason, and the cultivation of reason in woman, is alike friendly to the order of nature, and to private as well as public happiness" (Ditzion, 1967, pp. 29-30). The treatment of women had changed, but only to preserve her unequal relation to men. We cannot understand what love meant or was like without this recognition. We cannot appreciate how love changes without keeping this in mind.

Spiritual Intimacy: The Jacksonian Experience

We have seen how thoroughly personal life was embedded within public existence for colonial Americans. One's personal space was located within a clearly articulated and relatively stable social structure. Personal life was not private life. Personal identity and social stability were directly and mutually interdependent. In the nineteenth century this all changed. Rapid industrialization and the growth of urban centers transformed the social structure that had provided the context of social and personal life. The home ceased to be the center of all social existence. People's lives were divided between their work and their homes. There emerged around the family a sphere of private life that would have been unrecognizable to a visitor from colonial America.

At first glance, it is not immediately apparent that urbanization and industrial development bring about changes in the way people relate to one another. It is even less obvious how the changes in interpersonal relationships are tied to changes in social structure. Examination of the Jacksonian period suggests that changes in social structure require transformations at the most deeply personal levels of existence. Indeed, from our perspective one could almost say the social changes in the early decades of the nineteenth century created personal identity, and it is only along with the personal that it becomes necessary to speak of the "interpersonal."

In Jacksonian America both personal identity and interpersonal relations were in crisis. Large numbers of people were living in urban settings for which they were not, nor could they have been, prepared. Nissenbaum (1972) has described the situation of the person as follows:

> They were on their own, then, in mind and body. Reared as most of them must have been on farms and in small towns, they had been forced to leave by the pressures of population increase, insufficient or inadequate land, and competition from cheaper markets. . . . What loomed before them was not just a bleak future, but an *unknowable* future—and a far wider range of options than their parents had ever known, and for which nobody was equipped to prepare them. To remain at home might be to face a vicious circle of impoverishment; but to leave . . . actually created more problems than it solved: it introduced social arrangements, life-styles, daily routines, that were at the very least unsettling. Neighbors were unfamiliar; the new communities were often demographically skewed; the seasonal cycle of seed-time and harvest no longer served to regulate the rhythm of their lives; even their *bodies,* which had served to confirm their identity through the physical labor imposed by farm work, were useless and "alien" to the kind of activities demanded of them in colleges or cities. In such places people lived *in* their bodies, not *by* them, and indeed, those bodies—if not subdued—would themselves be part of the larger pattern of unpredictability and disorder in their lives. [P. 27]

It is as if there were an epidemic of identity crises, one that intensified as traditional institutions continued to be inappropriate to the uncertainties in peoples' lives. In colonial America, it often appeared that personal privacy was feared by society. In Jacksonian America, with the individual suddenly "free" of constant surveillance, personal privacy, at least initially, seems a threat to personal identity. Certainly some of the current literature on the effects of long term institutionalization (Goffman, 1962) supports such a notion. No longer under the watchful eyes of others, freed from the controlling influences of community shame and public punishment, people must have panicked at the flood of unchecked impulse that suddenly became their own responsibility. The following statement, written in 1833 by a New York City carpenter reflecting about his first experiences on his own, is representative of the response many people had to urban life:

I became excessively nervous, so that I was continually full of
apprehensions of danger, afraid of everything, and starting with
alarm at almost everything. If anything came upon me suddenly, it
affected me very much. . . . I often became so much embarrassed
and confused, that I would lose the power of speech; and
frequently, when in conversation, I used suddenly to lose my
thoughts in the midst of a sentence, and totally forgot what I was
talking about. . . . When out from home I was often attacked with
these turns in the street, and became so much confused and
bewildered, that it was with great difficulty that I could find my way
to my house. [Nissenbaum, 1972, p. 11]

The dilemma of these people, it seems, is that at the same time they
were threatened from within by their own impulses they were also
isolated from the very people from whom they had come to expect not
only restraint and control but warmth, intimacy, and in general the
gratification of emotional needs. There were, of course, a variety of ways
in which people attempted to satisfy these needs. Phrenology, special
diets, sexual restraint, regimented living arrangements—all can be
shown to have shared an emphasis on providing self-government, where
once the family and community had reigned. Many, of course, turned to
marriage. An institution rooted in the traditions of the communities
they had left behind, marriage must have promised to reestablish that
link with society that had been so abruptly severed. At the same time it
offered some of the emotional satisfactions people needed with
heightened urgency in the tough, uncaring environs of the city.
Particularly given the anonymity of the city, the possibility of being
known must have seemed very attractive. In addition, these were people
raised to live with others, not alone.

The popular literature of the time is filled with articles, advice, and
stories glorifying the family and the home as a utopian retreat (Jeffrey,
1972). These words, from an article entitled "Home" in an 1830 edition
of *Ladies Magazine*, capture quite well the popular middle-class opinion
of the time:

We go forth into the world, amidst scenes of business and of
pleasure; we mix with the gay and the thoughtless, we join the busy
crowd, and the *heart* is sensible to a desolation of feeling: we behold
every principle of justice and of honor, and even the dictates of
common honesty disregarded, and the delicacy of our moral sense is

wounded; we see the general good sacrificed to the advancement of personal interest; and we turn from such scenes, with a painful sensation, almost believing that virtue has deserted the abodes of men; again, we look to the *sanctuary* of *home*: there sympathy, honor, virtue, are assembled; there the eye may kindle with intelligence, and receive an answering glance; there disinterested love, is ready to sacrifice everything at the altar of affection. [Jeffrey, 1972, p. 28]

Of course we cannot take such a passage as an accurate description of the facts of domestic life. In fact, such glowing terms were necessitated to counteract the gloomy situation of the family at the time. Nissenbaum (1966) reports that the early 1800s produced an extraordinary increase in desertion rates, sufficient to warrant the granting of a special legal status to abandoned wives. It would seem that the problems city life imposed upon the individual were equally problems for the couple. Disconnected from the network of social relationships that characterized the colonial period, people were dependent upon one another for a depth and range of companionship that previously were provided by a diversity of people within community life. And as in the case of the individual person, it was not just satisfaction but control and support that community life offered. Cut off from this social support and restraint, couples had to generate the bases of their relationships from within the dynamic of their relationship and their personal feelings. If in colonial America relationships had provided the obligation of feeling, in the Jacksonian period feeling came to provide the reason for relationships. When feeling was gone, the relationship might end.

The coming together of two people became a private rather than a public matter, and so the formation of relationships had to be built on personal feelings. Consequently, along with the privatization of the family came the development of the realm of the interpersonal. Indeed, it was in the area of interpersonal relations that the range of self-consciousness and personal identity was expanded. The burgeoning of a whole popular literature addressing itself to this area attests to the special significance it acquired. The expansion of the realm of personal consciousness led to an increased interest in subjectivity. The early nineteenth-century glorification of romantic love was one major indicator of the new legitimacy of subjectivity (Nissenbaum, 1966;

Jeffrey, 1972). Still, it must be recognized that just as the colonial emphasis on the obligation to love acknowledged the tensions created by the intense intimacy of daily life, so we must suspect that the Jacksonians glorified the feelings of love when the conditions of daily existence made such feelings problematical. As we shall see shortly, there is ample evidence that this was the case.

First it must be noted, however, that the difficulties in interpersonal relations did not arise only because couples were no longer situated in stable, supportive communities. The differentiation of public from private that occurs within industrial development manifests itself in both individual consciousness and intimate relations. Industrialization separates the various spheres of social life. For the individual this means a fragmentation of efficacy. In preindustrial America work relations were somewhat personal, and personal relations were also work relations. There existed a relative harmony of the two within both person and society.

When work is moved outside of the home and the people with whom one works are no longer the people with whom one lives, there develop two fundamentally separate types of relationships. These relationships are defined within the boundaries of the separate institutions in which they occur; the dynamic of these relationships is determined by the functions of the institutions. Since the functions are different, a conflict between the styles of relationships required by the work place and home life is structured into the lives of all persons. These separate spheres of existence require different and often incompatible feelings, expectations, attitudes, interests, and behavior. Evidence of the conflict between the personal characteristics required by the separate domains of work and home can be seen in the advice given to their clients by phrenologists, predecessors of today's psychological testers and counselors. For example, Orson Fowler's (1859) analysis presented to an Edgar Hopkins contained the following:

> can manage work very well, are very reserved, need thawing out; Lack hope, must undertake more. . . .
> . . . have too much kindness, must be more selfish, trust people too much, don't endorse . . . need the softening influence of a woman, will be fond of traveling and always good in it. Very much need training from the female sex. Select for a wife a girl who

compliments, could not endure a scold. . . . your distinguishing trait will be good sound judgment . . . will succeed as a coal dealer.[1]

Clearly, those traits appropriate to success in the business world were generally incompatible with close personal relationships—restricted kindness, increased selfishness, and heightened distrust of others hardly are promotive of deep romantic love and sustained intimacy. The situation is further complicated by the fact that within developing industrial capitalism, the public sphere dominated the private. Consequently, occupational demands came to determine and shape the course of development of home life and intimate relationships. Much of the differentiation of roles that was a part of the changes of the nineteenth century was in direct response to the requisites of the work place and the reactions of people to those requisites. Because the quality and tone of existence in the work place were out of the direct or even indirect control of the great majority of people, personal existence became the province in which they could exercise their will and hope for some respite from the strains and deprecations of the world of work.

The idea of the home as utopian retreat was founded directly on the uncontrollable frustrations and indignities of the work world. At the same time, to become the person who could succeed at work required becoming a person in many ways incapable of warm and passionate intimate relationships. Given the intransigence of the public sphere, relations in the private domain were transformed so as to allow some degree of individual integrity and personal satisfaction to persons who needed to direct most of their energies to economic success. It was primarily through desexualization that this was accomplished.

The Jacksonian period marks the development of Victorian sexual morality in the United States. In this era, not only was sexual behavior severely restricted but sexual impulses were repressed as well. Colonial Americans had acknowledged sexual feelings as natural and restricted sexual behavior to marriage where it did not threaten social cohesion. Jacksonian Americans attempted to control the sexual impulses themselves. In so doing they transformed the nature and meaning of sexuality. Whereas sexual relations had previously been seen as naturally directed at obtaining sexual pleasure, they were now understood as legitimate only as an expression of warmth and intimacy, the ultimate

[1] Handwritten inscription.

indicator of a deep spiritual bond between people (Nissenbaum, 1966). All sexual release became suspect, and there emerged an extensive popular literature and active social campaigns against masturbation, prostitution, and all forms of excessive sexuality. It was not simple prudery that motivated these attacks on sexuality. Consider, for example, the following description of orgasm in the writings of Sylvester Graham. Graham was a major figure in the sex reform movement, the innovator of the popular Graham system of dietary regimen of nonirritating foods (of which the Graham cracker is our legacy), and manager of highly regimented boarding houses in which young men overwhelmed by the complications and ambiguities of urban life could find some structure around which to rebuild their lives (Nissenbaum, 1972). Graham wrote:

> The convulsive paroxysms attending venereal indulgence, are connected with the most intense excitement, and cause the most powerful agitation to the whole system that it is ever subject to. The brain, stomach, heart, lungs, liver, skin, and the other organs, feel it sweeping over them with the violence of a tornado. The powerfully excited and convulsed heart drives the blood, in fearful congestion, to the principal viscera,—producing oppression, irritation, debility, rupture, inflammation, and sometimes disorganization;—and this violent paroxysm is generally succeeded by great exhaustion, relaxation, lassitude, and even protraction. [Nissenbaum, 1972, p. 6]

Hardly an experience one would strive to obtain. Very simply, those people were afraid of sex. And it was not only the fanatics of the sex reform movement who expressed such fear. Even the most enlightened medical minds of the time recommended continence whenever possible. Medical studies had demonstrated that the loss of one ounce of semen was the equivalent of forty ounces of blood (Nissenbaum, 1972). Many doctors believed that sperm, if not released, was reabsorbed by the body and functioned as a nutrient. Even the phrenologists, for the time among the most accepting of sexuality, and willing to acknowledge that there was such a thing as sexual pleasure, argued against sexual gratification as an end in itself, separated from "virtuous love and wedlock." One of Fowler's (1840) works was entitled *Amativeness; or, Evils and Remedies of Excessive and Perverted Sexuality: including Warning and Advice to the Married and Single.* This work was a supplement to *Love and Parentage*, in which Fowler had written:

> Let then the libertine revel in his lustful, and therefore comparatively tasteless, pleasures, so soon to become the gall of bitterness to his innermost soul! Let the abandoned prostitute herself for gold—for a *living* even—but while the world stands, will the bed of lust be comparatively insipid . . . besides ultimately torturing the body and polluting the soul! Mistaken they, who expect happiness in either promiscuous indulgence or unbridled licentiousness. . . . How completely foolish the sensualist! Blasting the *very* pleasure he seeks! Bartering the most luxurious apple of paradise for the green, bitter, and poisonous grape of lust! [1839, p. 52]

He then went on to explain how only by the cooperation of amativeness with the intellect and moral sentiment could one rise above carnality, be consonant with one's true nature, and achieve the spiritual love that constituted real happiness.

Finally, examination of the sexual radicals of the period, the communards and free-love advocates, shows that even in rejecting monogamous marriage these nonconformists shared with the larger society a distrust of carnal sexuality. By no means were these people advocates or practitioners of orgiastic sexuality. Typically, sexual relations were carefully regulated and controlled, often toward the same goal—the maintenance of love and spiritual intimacy between people—that the dominant morality advocated (Kanter, 1972). The nonconformists argued that monogamous marriage was incompatible with sustained intimacy. Their sexual practices, however, mirrored the general dichotomy between spiritual and physical love. In the Oneida Community, for example, John Humphrey Noyes advocated "male continence" as the proper form of sexual intercourse (Kanter, 1972). In this technique the partners were motionless and they never, except when intending conception, achieved orgasm. Nissenbaum (1966) relates how Noyes justified this curious mixture of free love between consenting partners and restraint from sexual pleasure. Noyes distinguished between "amative" and "propagative" sexual acts, the first performed by the "organs of love or union," the second by the "organs of reproduction and procreation." If sexual intercourse were limited to the "conjunction of the organs of union," then "sexual intercourse becomes a purely social affair, the same in kind with other modes of kindly communion" (Nissenbaum, 1972, pp. 25–27). Noyes went so far as to show that physical pleasure was a component of procreation, not "union." This followed from the "fact" that

> The discharge of the semen and the pleasure connected with it, is not essentially social, since it can be produced in solitude. . . . The pleasure of the act is not produced by contact and interchange of life with the female, but by the action of the seminal fluid on the internal nerves of the male organ. [Nissenbaum, 1966, p. 27]

Even in free love, then, spiritual intimacy was the proper goal of sexual relations.

To summarize up to this point, on the surface it appears as if Jacksonian America continued the colonial rejection of sex outside of marriage. Closer examination reveals that the meaning and function of sexual relations both within and outside of marriage has been transformed so that the dominant middle-class attitude was that sexual relations were "a mode of sustaining deep and rich feelings of binding personal union between husband and wife" (Nissenbaum, 1966, p. 45). This transformation is part of a more general transformation in the meaning and function of interpersonal relations and the family. Whereas earlier the family had been the center of interrelated social institutions, now it had become a weak connecting link between the newly differentiated public and private realms. Precisely as it "decreased" in socioeconomic importance, the family now "increased" in psychological significance.

Thus far, we have focused on the problems these changes created within the newly emergent private sphere. However, the separation of the public from the private is no less a threat to social cohesion than it is to individual integrity and interpersonal intimacy. Each depends upon the other. Recall the degree to which colonial society undermined and restricted individual autonomy. When the personal is public rather than private, individual needs are easily subsumed within the requisites of social cohesion. The development of industrial capitalism required a relatively autonomous economic sphere, necessitating the separation of public and private. But a private sphere outside of the direct control of public institutions threatens social cohesion. There are many aspects to this threat and many perspectives from which it might be viewed. A particularly useful one for the purposes of the analysis presented here derives from the scheme developed by Philip Slater (1963) in his paper "On Social Regression." Elaborating some social implications of Freud's later instinct theory, Slater argues, "*so long as an individual cathects more than one object he will be unable to achieve a complete absence of libidinal tension,* and hence remain always available for collectivization" (p. 341).

Slater then proceeds to identify three specific threats to "aggregate maintenance," two of which, narcissistic withdrawal and dyadic withdrawal, are of special usefulness for the understanding of Jacksonian America. These concepts are almost self-explanatory. Narcissistic withdrawal is the "withdrawal of cathexis from all objects to the self"; dyadic withdrawal is the "withdrawal of cathexis from larger aggregates to a single intimate dyad" (p. 341). From this perspective we can understand the separation of the private from the public as greatly exacerbating the threat to social cohesion from both narcissistic and dyadic withdrawal. Urban and industrial development demanded strong and autonomous individuals and contained, self-sustaining couples. The emergence of an autonomous economic sphere creates the conditions for social disruption. At the same time, since personal identity is bound up with social structure, this disruption also threatens the integrity of individual identity. In discussing narcissistic withdrawal Slater observes:

> As a member of a collectivity, social anxiety is aroused in the individual by narcissistic withdrawal—by "satanic pride." But as a boundary-maintaining organism, instinctual anxiety is aroused in him when he observes a crime of passion or other manifestation of uncontrolled impulses. For the personality system evil resides in the id, while for the social system, it resides in the ego. [P. 346]

From this perspective, the near obsession with masturbation in the early nineteenth century makes a good deal of sense. In many ways masturbation is the epitome of narcissistic withdrawal. The masturbator is an eroticized caricature of the self-sufficient person. Victorian Americans condemned masturbation as self-abuse. Application of Slater's analysis suggests that they feared it as self-love. Suddenly there appeared in the 1830s a widely read literature warning against the harmful effects of onanism. Books such as *Solitary Vice Considered* made clear that both physical and mental health were endangered by masturbation (Nissenbaum, 1966, 1972). The notion of masturbatory insanity was prevalent, and mechanical devices designed to prevent children from in any way manipulating their genitals became popular (Nissenbaum, 1966). The campaign against masturbation, then, can be seen as serving the needs of both personal identity and social cohesion. Refraining from masturbation serves to control those impulses whose release threatens the person and simultaneously functions as a form of self-control that can substitute for the shattered external controls that previously guaranteed social cohesion. It could therefore be surmised that at least for Jacksonian Americans the strong ego is not an unambiguous evil. On the one hand, persons with strengthened individual egos threatened social cohesion to the extent that such persons were less responsible to others; Fowler's advice to Hopkins that he be less trusting, and so on, confirms this. At the same time, people reared within the strong community responsibility traditions of preindustrial America, and consequently dependent upon external rather than self control, were lacking the ego-strength required to be sufficiently self-denying to function effectively in the development of the autonomous economic sphere. This is a consequence of the fact that the demands of social cohesion and the demands of economic development were often contradictory. From the perspective developed here, the repression of masturbation in the early nineteenth century appears as an understandable response to new personal and social dilemmas.

Dyadic withdrawal presents an even greater threat to "aggregate maintenance" than does narcissistic withdrawal. Slater (1963) observes:

> An intimate dyadic relationship always threatens to short-circuit the libidinal network of the community and drain off its source of sustenance. The needs binding the individual to collectivities and reinforcing his allegiance thereto are now satisfied in the dyadic relationship, and the libido attached to these collectivities and diffused through their component members is drawn back and invested in the dyad. [P. 348]

We have already seen how in Jacksonian America the couple was released from the control and support of the larger social community, and how this created problems for interpersonal intimacy as well as personal identity. When we examine this phenomenon with Slater's optic, we see again that economic development creates the conditions that could potentially disrupt the social cohesion upon which further economic development must be dependent. When public and private life are divorced, there exists a need for an institution(s) that satisfies the unmet personal needs exacerbated by capitalism. These needs must be satisfied without threatening social dissolution as does dyadic withdrawal. Ideally such an institution should also serve the needs for personal identity. The trick is to locate individuals within intimate relationships that do not completely destroy the fragile but increasingly resilient boundaries of self-identity while simultaneously tying such intimate relationships back into the needs of the developing social system rather than the pleasures and satisfactions of the dyad. In many respects the emotionally based but sexually monogamous and de-eroticized marriages of Jacksonian America were ideally suited to these purposes. Slater presents an extended analysis of the ways in which the marriage ritual "becomes a series of mechanisms for pulling the dyad apart somewhat, so that its integration complements rather than replaces the various group ties of its members" (p. 353). The literature of the Jacksonian period is filled with references to the special importance of marriage and the family in determining the quality of social life. Crime, delinquency, poverty, and insanity were all linked to inadequacies of the family. Similarly, the well-ordered family was credited for economic success, social stability, and moral propriety (Rothman, 1971).

Kanter's (1972) analysis of the communal movement of the period can be taken as further demonstration of a generalized concern with social cohesion and uncertainty about the family's ability to create and sustain social order and community. Certainly the repression of sexuality—the psychological core of Victorian morality—was perfectly consonant with the need to establish a new base for the integration of the family with society. At the same time, desexualization probably served the needs of personal identity, not only through the process of impulse control but, additionally, by limiting the fusion that often accompanies intensified dyadic intimacy. Colonial Americans, although lacking sharply individualized identities, were not so threatened by dyadic fusion because of the diffusion of 'libido' throughout a multiplicity of relations. The separation of public and private spheres places opposing pressures on individual identity. Economic conditions were now favorable to autonomous individuals, while the intensified and expanded demands of the interpersonal subverted that autonomy and pushed toward fusion. Desexualization placed some limits on that fusion and therefore shored up the shaky identities of persons who had to fit together in many more ways than had couples earlier.

However, desexualization proceeded differently in men than in women. Victorian morality was constituted around a double standard for men and women. The base of this double standard was the redefinition of women as nonsexual beings. William Sanger, a respected physician, stated the dominant viewpoint as follows: "But it must be repeated and most decidedly, that without . . . stimulating cause (such as destitution, drink, or seduction and abandonment) the full force of sexual desire is seldom known to a virtuous woman. In the male sex, nature has provided a more susceptible organization than in the females" (Rugoff, 1971, p. 46). At the same time women were seen as innocent, the civilizing force juxtaposed against man's more animal nature, women's sexual transgressions were condemned more severely than those of men. Clearly, it was the desexualization that was new, not the unequal criteria against which men and women were judged.

Nissenbaum (1966) has suggested that Victorian morality should be viewed as "a creative response to circumstance." However creative, the logic behind the double standard of Victorian morality has been difficult to comprehend. Particularly puzzling is the fact that women as well as men voiced support for and attempted to live by this double standard.

The double standard is typically understood as a simple extension of male domination. I would like to suggest, rather, that the nineteenth-century double standard was the vehicle for a desexualization desired by men and women for opposing purposes. Men wanted to desexualize relationships to maintain their domination; women wanted to desexualize relationships to limit male domination. The relationship of desexualization to domination can best be understood in terms of the finer differentiation of sex roles in the nineteenth century.

The development of industry created a sexual division of labor that mirrored the essential features of the separation of the public from the private. Women were located in the private realm, men in the public. When work left the home, so did men. Women were left behind managing the affairs of the home and caring for and raising the children (recall that we are speaking in this paper of the middle class). It was in the 1830s that books giving advice on "domestic economy" and child-rearing principles became popular. It was only in the 1800s that children began to come under the authority of women. Until the nineteenth century, children, although cared for by women, were seen as under the authority of the man, and women, no matter who was at fault, never received custody of children in cases of divorce (Flexner, 1959). In the nineteenth century, women's energies were directed, with unprecedented intensity, toward the raising of their children. Simultaneously, men's energies were directed toward the development of autonomy and the achievement of economic success. Recall the concern of Jacksonian men with the preservation of energy, and the equation of loss of sperm with debility. Recall also the glorification of spiritual love. Perhaps separating sexual from emotional love allowed men to "reinvest" their "unspent" sexual energies (the nineteenth-century euphemism for orgasm is "spend" [Nissenbaum, 1966]) in the world of work. However, simply pulling back from sexuality would have created additional problems for men because, traditionally, sexuality and domination had been fused, as our examination of colonial America illustrated. A unilateral rejection of sexuality would have been tantamount to abdication of male authority. Hence, the only way to preserve male domination while still reducing the pressures of sexual expectations was to redefine women as asexual creatures, or at least as less sexual than men.

Ironically, such a redefinition of the sexual nature of women was compatible with the attempts of early nineteenth-century women to curb male authority and redefine sexual roles. Carol Smith-Rosenberg (1973) suggests that many of the women participants in the moral reform movement were reacting to the inferior position of women in Jacksonian America and against male domination. Women

> had few rights and little power. Their role in society was passive and sharply limited. Women were ... denied formal education ... [seen as] inadequate to sustained intellectual effort ... denied the vote. ... Professional roles ... were closed to women. ... Most economic alternatives to marriage ... were closed to women. Their property rights were still restricted and females were generally considered to be the legal wards of either the state or of their nearest male relative. [Smith-Rosenberg, 1973, p. 563]

Smith-Rosenberg suggests that "such women channeled frustration, anger and a compensatory sense of superior righteousness into the reform movement" (p. 564). She goes on to discuss the way in which the moral reform movement attacked the double standard by demanding equal treatment of men and women. However, while attacking the double standard, the women of the moral reform movement exploited and accepted the image it presented of woman as asexual innocent. The *Advocate,* the weekly of the Female Moral Reform Society,

> entertained several primary assumptions concerning the nature of human sexuality. Perhaps most central was the conviction that women felt little sexual desire; they were in almost every instance induced to violate the Seventh Commandment by lascivious men who craftily manipulated not their sensuality, but rather the female's trusting and affectionate nature. A woman acted out of romantic love, not carnal desire; she was innocent and defenseless, gentle and passive. . . . The male lecher on the other hand was a creature controlled by base sexual drives which he neither could nor would control. He was . . . powerful and decisive; unwilling . . . to curb his own willfulness, he callously used it to coerce the more passive and submissive female. [Smith-Rosenberg, 1973, p. 571]

Whatever their intent, the moral reformers' demand for desexualization meshed well with the needs of Jacksonian men to limit their investment in intimate relations and maintain their domination. Simultaneously, this desexualization of the husband-wife relation probably allowed for the redirection of women's repressed sexual energies to the relationship with her children. Since at the same time, desexualization also served the male and female need for impulse control and was compatible with the socially needed limitations on dyadic withdrawal, we can see Victorian morality as a quite creative response to social conditions.

Intimacy: The Progressive Era

Michael Katz (1968) has said of those who experienced the changes of urbanization and industrialization that they "watched the contours of society propelled, twisted, and bent into radically new shapes, shapes that brought new forms to all aspects of the life of men, to their every relation" (p. 5). These changes expanded and continued throughout the nineteenth century, transforming the lives of increasing numbers of people. Richard Sennett's (1970) study of urban life in the last third of the nineteenth century, *Families against the City,* illustrates sharply how, "For men confused and scared by the new city, the family offered an intimate world with an internal binding power of its own. . . . men tried to survive in the city by holding on to what they did in work—and concentrated their involvement and emotional capacities in the intimate area of wife and child" (pp. 196–97).

By the turn of the century, the altered social patterns that the Victorians had taken to be signs of the disintegration of the family were recognized as indicators of adjustment to the living conditions associated with urban life and industrial development (Kennedy, 1970). In 1909, one commentator observed, "The old economic framework of the family has largely fallen away, leaving more of the strain on the personal tie" (Kennedy, 1970, p. 39). And Arthur Calhoun (1919), writing a social history of the American family, noted the degree to which Americans were "placing the entire burden of securing the success of marriage and the family life upon the characters and capacities of two persons. . . . American marriage is a union of two people and not an alliance between two families" (p. 169).

The second decade of the twentieth century has been described as the "first years of our own time" in the classic study of that period, *The End of American Innocence* (May, 1959). Enormous amounts have been written about that period. It is my impression that intimate relations retained the shape they had assumed during the Jacksonian era. Basically, attitudes and ideas were finally catching up with a reality which had begun to form in the early nineteenth century. To be sure, there were changes in the early years of the twentieth century, but not of the same magnitude as those which initially accompanied industrialization. This discussion will focus particularly on two features of middle-class interpersonal relationships during that period—the increased acceptance of personal fulfillment as a goal of relationships and the reemergence of repressed sexuality.

The problems that were unprecedented traumas for the first generations of urban pioneers were familiar difficulties for many early twentieth-century city dwellers. Various institutions such as compulsory education, modifications in child-rearing practices, and reductions in family size had resulted in more autonomous and individuated persons. Those who successfully mastered both themselves and the domain of work became the respectable middle-class men of the last third of the nineteenth century.

Certainly, the emergence of psychology and much of its early content (e.g., William James, 1890) bears witness to the development of personal identity. Dewey (1887), author of the first textbook of scientific psychology, defined the discipline as "the science of the facts or phenomena of the self" (p. 3). The goal of these selves was quite clear. C. H. Judd (1907) asserted: "The individual must seek of his own initiative those higher forms of organization which will most fully realize the possibilities of his life. The highest level of individual organization is reached when mental development becomes a matter of voluntary control" (p. 324).

As it first developed, this ideal referred primarily to men. Within the middle class, the sexual division of labor imposed a sharp differentiation of male and female sex roles. Confined to the home and the tasks of nurturance of both her children and her husband, the ideal American woman was an innocent and helpless creature who existed to please others rather than herself. In *Why Women Are So*, Mary Roberts Coolidge compared women to an actor who,

> like the woman, makes his place in life chiefly by the cultivation of manner and appearance. He, like her, depends for success upon pleasing rather than being admirable. The "matinee idol" is an extreme example of character—or, rather, perversion of character— by the social necessity of being charming and of trading in assumed emotions. [Kennedy, 1970, p. 53]

There is a subtle irony here. One of the consequences of desexualization, isolation of the family, and the economic pressures of urban industrial life is a reduction of family size. This in turn leads to an intensification and individuation of husband-wife (and parent-child) relationships. Once the initial traumas of uncontrolled impulse have been handled, couples expect a good deal of one another to sustain the mutual interest and attraction necessary to preserve the emotional tie that is the cement of the relationship. For women, this required a degree of cultivation and education previously denied them. One woman, Lydia Commander, around the turn of the century put it this way: "In the old days, a married woman was supposed to be a frump and a bore and a physical wreck. Now you are supposed to keep up intellectually, to look young and well and be fresh and bright and entertaining" (Kennedy, 1970, p. 40). The increased sophistication and education which women required to remain "suitable" companions for their more worldly men necessarily heightened their own self-consciousness. Simultaneously, the male role had developed in ways so different from that of females that men were particularly impoverished in the emotional and interpersonal dimensions—these had become women's province in the sexual division of labor. We have already seen how repressed and limited was the narcissism of the manly Victorian man. Necessarily then, the woman's role as a reflection of her man must have been an unsatisfactory one. There can be little pleasure in playing mirror to a person not in touch with his own narcissism.

Women's growing self-consciousness was not only a private matter. The feminist movement, no longer confined to attempts to alter the legal status of women, concerned itself directly with the nature of female character. The transformation of the feminine personality became a goal for the women of that decade. Self-actualization became a legitimate aspiration. In politicizing the problems of the personal lives of women, feminists pointed to an opposition between society and self, and criticized the repressive nature of sex-role socialization. The demands and criticisms raised by the feminists did not go unanswered. Kennedy reports how the opponents of feminism often based their attacks on the alleged selfishness of the new women. For example, in 1909 Anna Rodgers was able to explain the failure of American marriages as the result of women's involvement in "the latter-day cult of individualism; the worship of the brazen calf of Self" (Kennedy, 1970, p. 48). Such accusations were particularly ironic because the feminists themselves were critical of the individualism of the time and often attributed the responsibility for selfishness to the institution of marriage and the family.

At any rate, personal identity and interpersonal life were becoming public matters. We have already explored some of the ways in which the development of industrial capitalism was based on the separation of the public from the private; private needs came to be shaped by the requisites of economic development. The issues raised by the feminists focused critical attention on the impoverishment of personal life. Such criticism has the potential to expand into a general critique of social relations and the social structure. That social structure can be bolstered by reducing the opposition between public and private spheres, by de-privatizing identity. When people's personal needs can be aligned with the priorities of economic development, demands for personal fulfillment can support the dominant social order. Social cohesion is then served rather than threatened by personal fulfillment. Feminists experienced the need to redefine personal identity. Business dominated the process of redefinition. The first steps toward this redefinition were well under way in the 1920s. John C. Burnham (1968) has observed:

> One of the striking developments of the 1920's was the culmination on a mass scale of public interest in personal, introspective accounts of private experiences. A mass market for popularized personal documents grew primarily out of two sources: the lovelorn column of the newspaper and the cult of physical, that is bodily, development. As a matter of fact, it was the editors of *Physical Culture*, the ... health and exercise magazine, who initiated the phenomenon. Their offices had been flooded by unsolicited letters of essentially confessional nature that contained the details of intimate secrets. The editors got the idea of publishing them, and *True Story Magazine* was born. Its success was immediate and unbelievable, and a host of imitators sprang up. [P. 368]

It was not only by transforming personal problems to commercial products and public entertainment that the larger social order reasserted its control of personal life. Personal fulfillment itself was equated with consumption.

As the economy that had undermined the productive role of the house and family in society continued to expand, it transformed the nature of domestic life as well. The period between 1914 and 1924 saw huge increases in the sale of canned goods, and comparable increases in the use of commercial laundries (Horton, 1973). At the same time, the number of appliances such as electric irons, washing machines, and vacuum cleaners doubled and tripled. There were large economic stakes in keeping women at home, and magazines such as *Good Housekeeping* and *Harper's Bazaar*, as well as the advertising industry and the home economist movement, combined to create the image of homemaking as a profession; "by 1920 the woman did not have to step outside her door to be an administrator or an executive; her house was a plant with its equipment, and she was the director of personnel" (Horton, 1973). Christopher Lasch (1965) has termed this the "pseudo-feminism" response.

The fulfillment that was available for the woman who accepted marriage was that of a consumer, cut off from direct spontaneous action in the world. It was a curious fulfillment, based on the denial of self as actor and the deception that consuming was acting. The more radical feminists, such as Charlotte Perkins Gilman and Olive Schreiner, decried this development toward what they called "parasitism." They called on women to give up the luxuries and leisure of consumerism (Lasch, 1965). For the feminists complete fulfillment could come only through active experience. Lasch (1965) saw in early feminism a reaction to the "eventlessness" of the life of the middle-class woman.

> She said no more than what every intellectual of the age . . . suspected, that his own class had somehow lost contact with life. To live fully, directly, spontaneously; to live to the outer limits of one's capacities; to immerse oneself in the stream of experience— all this was no longer something one took for granted as the essence of the human condition, but had become rather an objective to be strived after with all one's powers. . . . It was precisely this mystical sense of the sanctity of experience, life, growth, and development that rendered the men and women of the period incapable of setting up an alternative to the cult of self-fulfillment the destructive possibilities of which they were so quick to discern. Charlotte Gilman could deplore the unbridled individualism which she saw as the curse of modern society and at the same time insist that personal "growth" was the law of life and the only goal worth pursuing. [1965, p. 63]

But to pursue personal growth it was necessary for women to alter social conditions—particularly the differences in opportunities for men and women. For most women the jobs available were hardly an attractive alternative to the newly elevated homemaking "profession." Employment and career opportunities for women were tightly restricted, severely underpaid, and generally unpromising and unrewarding. For example, in 1919 women were excluded from more than half of all civil service exams, and men were paid almost twice what women were for comparable work (Horton, 1973).

For many women work became a way station prior to marriage. Popular magazines were filled with stories that presented the office as the setting for passionate romance, and the job as the means of meeting an "attractive" mate. If the experiences available to women were to promise personal growth, it was necessary to eliminate the inequality between men and women. There was a bind, however. In struggling for equality, women necessarily pointed to the many ways they were victimized as women, particularly in relation to men. Lasch (1965) has suggested that in appealing to their victimization the feminists unwittingly reverted to a theme that was only barely a variant of the traditional notion of woman as helpless innocent. He cites the campaign for changes in the divorce laws as an example: "it was not the image of women as equals that inspired the reform of the divorce laws, but the image of women as victims. . . . woman depended on a sentimentalization of womanhood which eroded the idea of equality as easily as it promoted it" (1965, p. 59). There was, however, one way out of this dilemma for some women—to get out of or stay out of relationships with men, particularly traditional relationships with their stereotyped sex-role expectations. Having been socialized to meet those expectations, some women found it necessary to avoid the traditional roles and relationships of women, in order to move toward self-fulfillment. Lasch notes that several feminist leaders such as Sanger and Gilman had to leave their marriages before they could come into their own.

Clearly, for both feminists and nonfeminists, fulfillment was represented in the new expectations women could hold for their lives and the new demands they might place on relationships. It was the definition of that fulfillment and the content of those expectations that separated feminists from nonfeminists.

It was not only around the issue of consumerism that questions about the fulfillment of the new woman arose. One of the most striking features of the second decade of the twentieth century was the reemergence of the sexuality that had been so thoroughly repressed throughout the Victorian era. Civilized morality required a denial of sexual feelings as well as restrictions on sexual behavior. When the feminists raised questions about the degree to which sex dominated all aspects of social life they were referring to gender, not erotic sexuality. It is particularly interesting, then, that it was precisely when women had begun to question the overriding social significance of gender that their erotic sexuality was rediscovered, encouraged, and developed. Women changed drastically, in appearance and behavior. Between the years 1913 and 1928 the amount of material needed for an average dress diminished from nineteen and a quarter yards to seven yards (Horton, 1973). An examination of the styles of dress alone would show the changes from restraint to release. There were equally striking changes in sexual behavior. One of the first studies of sexual behavior found that women born before the turn of the century had much less sexual experience (both pre- and post-marriage) than did those women born after

(Hamilton & MacGowan, 1929). These results were later confirmed in Kinsey's (1953) report that almost all the increase in frequency of sexual behavior of women occurred between 1916 and 1930.

A multiplicity of factors, too numerous to integrate into this discussion, went into the reemergence of female sexuality and the legitimation of sexual pleasure. Among these was psychoanalysis. Freud had visited America in 1909, and his impact was tremendous, coming as he did in the midst of great uncertainty about sex roles and sexuality. There is often a great disparity between Freud's writings and the psychoanalytic literature that became popular in the United States (Hale, 1971). Both formal psychoanalytic works and the popularized psychoanalysis of the "new psychology" converged on the conclusion that the repression of sexual impulses was "bad." In liberating erotic sexuality at a time when the question of self-fulfillment loomed large in the consciousness of both critics and defenders of the social order, psychoanalysis facilitated the equation of sexual gratification with self-fulfillment. Kennedy (1970) offers an interesting observation about Freud's effect.

> Freud did not so much start a revolution as rechannel one already in progress. William James and others in the nineteenth century had identified the inner self with the emotions. Freud superimposed on that view the idea that all emotion—indeed all psychic life—sprang from sexuality, and therefore that the self was defined by sexuality. [Pp. 68–69]

Although this interpretation somewhat distorts both James and Freud, it is a distortion that seems to have been made in most of the then popular discussions of psychoanalysis, self, and sexuality. As Kennedy points out, Freudian psychology provided an answer to the question of "the nature of the female personality." Women were passive and irrational, their nature grounded in sexually bound, instinctually determined psychological needs. In this way psychoanalytic thought, however incorrectly understood, allowed for an updating of the female personality through the emergence of sexuality and a continuation of the notion of a biologically based woman's nature. Simultaneously this change preserved the balance of power between men and women without too severely threatening social cohesion. Women were free to seek fulfillment, so long as it was within the boundaries of their sexuality. The flapper who emerged in the 1920s confirmed her self-worth in her value as a sexual object. Burnham (1968) describes the tone of the early twenties as narcissistic. Recalling Slater's analysis, "Narcissistic withdrawal . . . combined with a weak ego . . . is impotent as a social force" (1963, p. 348). From this perspective we can understand the changes that occurred in the "first years of our time" as changes in which women were channeled toward narcissistic withdrawal rather than developing strong egos. Keep in mind as well the popular image in the twenties of the professional woman as a de-eroticized woman. Hamilton and MacGowan's (1929) study found that wives who were not working described themselves as more happily married than those who were and that the type of woman who seeks a job outside the home is a sexually subnormal type. Steven Marcus (1969) suggests that a masculine fear of impotence along with the fear of sexual impulse underlay the repressed sexuality of Victorian morality. To the extent that this fear was shared by American men, it may be that the reemergence of sexuality, signaling as it did that sexual impulse was not intrinsically aggressive and antisocial, served to diminish for men the fear of impotence. The double standard, although it had served masculine needs when it originated, had come to present numerous problems for men as well as women (Cominos, 1963).

Finally, it must be mentioned that the reemergence of sexuality also served the larger economic needs to transform the home to a self-conscious center of consumption. There developed after World War I new modes in advertising, as the advertisement came not only to inform people of product availability but also to create and manipulate product needs. Modern advertising attempted to equate product consumption with self-fulfillment, and one of the major manipulations with which this equation was created was the eroticization of commodities. The emerging advertising industry borrowed many of its ideas, and bought many of its personnel, from the ranks of the psychological professions. In this way, the sexuality that surfaced early in the twentieth century did not remain the possession of the couples who experienced it. Sexuality rather rapidly became public property and served to undercut the accentuated threat of dyadic withdrawal that was represented by sexual intimacy.

Of course it is necessary to recognize that there is a great difference between the release of sexuality and the fulfillment of its potentiality. We know now how far from satisfactory were those newly legitimated sexual relations. We know too that attitudes and values change slowly, and that even as sexual behavior had changed, people were not always easy with even their own behaviors. Nonetheless, these changes are significant ones, and they prepare us for an examination of our own time.

Technological Intimacy: The Contemporary Experience

As in earlier times, the future of marriage is uncertain, the value of intimacy appears subverted, and the meaning of sexuality confused. I will not even begin to cite the innumerable books and articles addressing the future of marriage (Bernard, 1972), the nature of love (Rubin, 1973), the means to creative divorce (Krantzler, 1973), the liberation of sexuality (Bengis, 1972), and so on. Nor would I be foolish enough to attempt to make sense of all these problems. Rather, I would like to draw from the historical record, merely to identify a few continuities in those phenomena—particularly those continuities that appear to us as changes—locate these phenomena within the analysis developed here, and suggest some cautions about the directions in which our work and our relationships are developing. I begin convinced of two things: (1) That what appears to be the disintegration of a past mode of relationship is often only a transformation of that mode. Our social relations, since they develop more slowly than the economic sphere that dominates them, come eventually to be appropriate to the conditions in which we exist. (2) That what appears to be a liberation from past oppression is often only a transformation of that oppression. The changing needs that we experience in our social relations are most often tied to the changing needs of the economic domain.

We entered the 1920s having temporarily averted the questions raised by the feminists. They had asked, in the most general sense, if and how social relations and self-fulfillment were related. They raised the question of whether or not interpersonal intimacy and self-development were compatible. Such a question could not be fully answered before sexuality itself was legitimated within relationships. If we see as one of the results of the last fifty years the legitimation of sexuality, we can understand somewhat better how we have returned to the question of the relationship between intimacy and self-fulfillment. In a certain sense then, we can say that sexuality has been "liberated" in that (1) it can be rather openly acknowledged and valued; and (2) it no longer seems confined to the sanctioned relationship of marriage. It is not enough, however, to observe that sexuality is liberated. We need to ask as well, "How has it been liberated, and toward what ends?" Let us briefly retrace the history of this "liberation."

In the nineteenth century emotional intimacy was severed from sexual pleasure. Sexual intercourse was accepted as an expression of and means to emotional intimacy. By itself, sexual pleasure was seen as demeaning the love between two people. Beginning in the early years of the twentieth century, sexual pleasure was readmitted to meaningful intimate relationships and accepted as a part of that intimacy. Specifically, sexual pleasure was accepted as an aspect of self-fulfillment and self-fulfillment acknowledged as an acceptable purpose of intimate relationships. In turn, these relationships had to function to satisfy people for whom the notion of self-fulfillment had been greatly expanded. However, sexual intercourse was still taken as an indicator of emotional intimacy. Consequently, once sexual pleasure was legitimated, sexual intercourse took on more emotional significance in relationships and sexual pleasure became the indicator of emotional intimacy.

Consider the way in which the so-called recent liberation of sexuality has proceeded—primarily by again separating sexual pleasure from emotional intimacy, by lessening the importance of sexual relations. Almost all of the practices by which sexuality is brought into so-called open relationships depend on limiting the emotional meaning of sexuality in both the primary and secondary relationships. At the same time that sexuality is made to mean less in relationships, it is still taken as a measure of self-fulfillment and advocated as the means to such.

Think also of the terms in which sexuality has been "liberated"—primarily by transforming that sexuality, once it is severed from social relations, into a technological skill. Thus we develop manuals to teach sexual techniques, and therapeutic programs to reeducate those whose technical training was inadequate. It is not only sexuality that is so transformed—sensitivity and encounter groups, human relations training, and other institutions have also developed. These too can be seen as a further reduction of the interpersonal to the technological (Koch, 1971). These too remove emotionality from the social relations in which it originates and relocate it in the realm of skill. Thus, we observe that at the same time that sexuality is severed from emotionality both are reduced to technical skill.

One needs to question how, if sexuality is accepted because its significance is reduced, it can serve as a means of self-fulfillment? And if it does so function, who are the selves for whom such sexuality is self-fulfilling? Are they persons who see and experience themselves as conglomerates of technical skills, obtaining satisfaction in the proficiency of their performance? Certainly one might question whether these changes are rightly called liberation.

Slater cites Alexander's remark that "*the erotic value of an action is inversely related to the degree to which it loses the freedom of choice and becomes coordinated* and subordinated to other functions and becomes a part of an organized system, of a goal structure" (1963, p. 350). My fear is that the seeming liberation of sexuality has occurred because sex has become coordinated and subordinated to that organized system, and a part of the goal structure of the most recent developments of corporate capitalism. Among those goals is the reintegration of the public and the private. At that level of abstraction, this goal neither threatens nor supports the social structure. It can be held by both critics and supporters of this system. The significant issue is on what terms this reintegration will take place. If the terms by which we understand both our personal identities and our most intimate relationships become the terms of the technological economy that dominates our lives, then we will participate, as have numerous generations before us, in making ourselves over into the beings that system needs us to be. Slater also cites Freud's remark in *Group Psychology and the Analysis of the Ego*:

> Two people coming together for the purpose of sexual satisfaction, insofar as they seek for solitude, are making a demonstration against . . . the group feeling. The more they are in love, the more completely they suffice for each other. . . .
>
> Even in a person who has in other respects become absorbed in a group the *directly sexual tendencies preserve a little of his individual activity.* [Slater, 1963, p. 351]

Perhaps sexuality and emotionality are "defused" by removing them from their organic base in social relations and relocating them in the repertoire of individual technical skills. This is not to argue against teaching people about sexuality and sexual technique. There are ways in which technical training is potentially liberating. But technical training by itself, severed from social relations, directs people toward performance, not fulfillment. Once sexual relations become performances, sexuality no longer threatens to promote dyadic withdrawal. Rather, in Alexander's words, sexual behavior "becomes coordinated and subordinated to other functions." If this analysis is correct it suggests that sexuality will lose its "erotic value" and the "sexual tendencies" will be unable to preserve individuality. Rather, sexual activity will become a means of reabsorbing the person into the group. This analysis complements Marcuse's discussion of the effects of the sexualization of the work world, a phenomenon he designates as repressive desublimation.

> It has often been noted that advanced industrial civilization operates with a greater degree of sexual freedom—"operates" in the sense that the latter becomes a market value and a factor of social mores. Without ceasing to be an instrument of labor the body is allowed to exhibit its sexual features in the everyday work world and in work relations. . . . The sexy office and sales girls, the handsome, virile junior executive and floor walker are highly marketable commodities. [Marcuse, 1964, p. 74]

There are other ways as well in which the criteria and values of the economic sphere permeate the interpersonal and personal under the guise of liberation. Consider the conception of intimate relationships represented by the modern, "personalized" marriage contract. Jan Dizard (1974) has observed how the increasingly common practice of writing specific contracts for marriages, while it appears to make explicit the rights and obligations, duties and expectations of the "partners," represents a further incursion of the values and conceptions of the business world into the interpersonal. Contracts are necessary in the business world, because the parties must assume each other interested in and motivated by self-interest in the most narrow sense of that term. Presumably a business relationship progresses as long as it continues to serve the narrow self-interest of the contracting persons. Similarly, these personalized marriage contracts stipulate the continuation of the marriage as long as it continues to serve the narrow self-interest of the marriage "partners." One might wonder whether such an orientation to marriage precludes the possibility of an "unselfish" love. Some might argue that the historical record provides ample reason to distrust the "costs" of interpersonal intimacy, particularly for women. Still it hardly seems that the writing of contracts has made the business world a model to emulate for personal relationships. Interestingly, in a recent study

Eric Strauss (1974) found that both partners in successful marriages shared a sense of their relationship as encompassing their personal self-fulfillment rather than contradicting it. Simultaneously, they often were able to tolerate some degree of self-sacrifice for the sake of the relationship. It is also of interest that these couples seemed to share a "work orientation" toward their relationships.

The analysis developed here suggests that we should return to the questions raised by the early feminists: How are we to define self-fulfillment? What is the relationship between intimacy and self-fulfillment? These are, of course, enormous questions. They are anchored in our conception of the person and our beliefs about social relations. I suspect we still think of the person as indivisible, we still imagine fulfillment as occurring in spite of rather than through social relations. I believe our culture creates persons for whom what appears as self-actualization and genuinely satisfying relationships with others are incompatible. This was recognized many years ago by Karen Horney (1937), when she spoke of the "neurotic personality of our time." By this she meant "not only . . . that there are neurotic persons having essential peculiarities in common, but also that these basic similarities are essentially produced by the difficulties existing in our time and culture" (p. 34). She went on to discuss how, because of systematic features of our culture, "the great majority of us have to struggle with problems of competition, fears of failure, emotional isolation, distrust of others and of our own selves" (p. 34). One of the main features of the personality who emerged from the struggle with these problems was the "neurotic need for affection."

> We all want to be liked and to feel appreciated, but in neurotic persons the dependence on affection or approval is disproportionate to the real significance which other persons have for their lives. Although we all wish to be liked by persons of whom we are fond, in neurotics there is an indiscriminate hunger for appreciation or affection, regardless of whether they care for the person concerned or whether the judgment of that person has any meaning for them . . . there is a marked contradiction between their wish for affection and their own capacity for feeling or giving it. [Pp. 36-37]

In the context established here, we could reinterpret the neurotic need for affection as the modal response to the "competition, fears of failure, emotional isolation, distrust of others and of our own selves." In other words, from this reading it would appear that we have asked more of relationships than they can give. This is precisely what defines a neurotic response. We were attempting to satisfy in personal relationships needs that did not originate in and could not be satisfied by those relationships. Relationships so burdened necessarily fail, and in failing they exacerbate the sense of emotional isolation, distrust of others and ourselves, and so forth, from which people seek release and relief. From this perspective, the tendency today to make relationships "mean" less can be seen as a "more realistic" assessment of the potentialities of interpersonal intimacy. However, this overlooks the fact that the demands that had been placed on intimate relationships were themselves important and legitimate; it was only inappropriate to expect that they could be met by love and intimacy. It appears that the direction in which we are moving today means abandoning those demands and settling for less, for what we can get. What we can get are commodities, and we have moved toward a new form of consumerism in which the products consumed are other persons who are appreciated in terms of their ability to satisfy our fragmented needs. The personal sections of our newspapers and periodicals are filled with advertisements for these commodities. Computer matching, mate swapping, and "sensitivity" weekends all participate in this transformation of persons into commodities. In this way we come also to ask too little of social relations. Ultimately I think we must turn to a restructuring of society. The needs that have led us to ask both too much and too little of social relations have not disappeared, nor will they. Clearly, a social structure does not guarantee the actualization of persons. Certainly the elimination of economic and sexual inequality, the abolition of alienated labor are not the same as satisfying, passionate, and loving relations. But I cannot believe that such relations are possible between people who are not free to be equals.

References

Bendix, R. *Tradition and modernity reconsidered.* Institute of Industrial Relations and Institute of International Studies. Berkeley, Calif., 1968.

Bengis, I. *Combat in the erogenous zone.* New York: Knopf, 1972.

Bernard, J. *The future of marriage.* New York: World, 1972.

Burnham, J. C. The new psychology: From narcissism to social control. In J. Braeman, R. H. Bremmer,& D. Brady (Eds.), *Change and continuity: The 1920's.* Columbus: Ohio University Press, 1968.

Calhoun, A. *A social history of the American family*, vol. 3. New York: Barnes & Noble, 1919.

Cominos, P. J. Late Victorian respectability and the social system. *International Review of Social History*, 1963, *8*, 18–48; 216–250.

Demos, J. *A little commonwealth: Family life in Plymouth Colony.* New York: Oxford University Press, 1970.

Dewey, J. *Psychology.* New York: Harper & Bros., 1887.

Ditzion, S. *Marriage, morals, and sex in America: A history of ideas.* New York: Octagon Press, 1967.

Dizard, J. Personal communication, 1974.

Flaherty, D. *Privacy in colonial New England.* Charlottesville: University of Virginia Press, 1967.

Flexner, E. *Century of struggle.* Cambridge: Harvard University Press, 1959.

Fowler, O. S. *Love and parentage.* New York: Fowler & Wells, 1839.

Fowler, O. S. *Amativeness.* New York: Fowler & Wells, 1840.

Fowler, O. S. *New illustrated self-instructor in phrenology and physiology.* New York: Fowler & Wells, 1859.

Goffman, E. *Asylums.* New York: Doubleday, 1962.

Hale, N. G., Jr. *Freud and the Americans.* New York: Oxford University Press, 1971.

Hamilton, G. V., & MacGowan, K. *What is wrong with marriage?* New York: A. & C. Boni, 1929.

Horney, K. *The neurotic personality of our time.* New York: Norton, 1937.

Horton, R. Freedom or facade? A study of sex roles and stereotypes in the 1920's. Manuscript, University of Massachusetts, Amherst, 1973.

James, W. *The principles of psychology.* New York: Henry Holt, 1890.

Jeffrey, K. The family as utopian retreat from the city. In S. Tessele (Ed.), *The family, communes and utopian societies.* New York: 1972.

Judd, C. H. *Psychology.* New York: C. Scribner's Sons, 1907.

Kanter, R. M. *Commitment and community.* Cambridge: Harvard University Press, 1972.

Katz, M. *The irony of early school reform.* Boston: Beacon Press, 1968.

Kennedy, D. *Birth control in America.* New Haven: Yale University Press, 1970.

Kinsey, A. *Sexual behavior in the human female.* Philadelphia: Saunders, 1953.

Koch, S. The image of man in encounter groups. *Journal of Humanistic Psychology*, 1971, *11*, 109–128.

Krantzler, M. *Creative divorce.* New York: Evans, 1973.

Lasch, C. *The new radicalism in America, 1889-1963: The intellectual as social type.* New York: Vintage Press, 1965.

Marcus, S. *The other Victorians: A study of sexuality and pornography in mid-nineteenth century England.* New York: Basic Books, 1969.

Marcuse, H. *One dimensional man.* Boston: Beacon Press, 1964.

May, H. F. *The end of American innocence.* New York: Quadrangle Press, 1959.

Morgan, E. *The Puritan family: Religion and domestic relations in seventeenth century New England.* (revised ed.) New York: Harper & Row, 1966.

Nissenbaum, S. W. From pleasure to intimacy: The glorification of sexual love in early Victorian America, 1830-1860. Manuscript, University of Massachusetts, Amherst, 1966.

Nissenbaum, S. W. Sex reform and social change, 1830–1840. Paper presented to the
    American Historical Association, 1972.

O'Neill, N., & O'Neill, G. *Open marriage.* New York: Evans, 1972.

Rothman, D. V. *The discovery of the asylum: Social order and disorder in the new republic.*
    Boston: Little, Brown, 1971.

Rubin, Z. *Liking and loving.* New York: Holt, Rinehart, & Winston, 1973.

Rugoff, M. *Prudery and passion.* New York: Putnam, 1971.

Sennett, R. *Families against the city: Middle class homes of industrial Chicago, 1872–1890.*
    Cambridge: Harvard University Press, 1970.

Slater, P. E. On social regression. *American Sociological Review,* 1963, *38,* 339–363.

Smith-Rosenberg, C. Beauty, the beast, and the militant woman: A case study in sex roles
    and social stress in Jacksonian America. *American Quarterly,* 1973, pp. 562–584.

Strauss, E. Couples in love. Ph.D. dissertation, University of Massachusetts, 1974.

4
Needed Research on Commitment in Marriage
PAUL C. ROSENBLATT

Research is needed on the internal states and external factors that influence people to stay together. One way of approaching the problem area is through the concept of commitment. In this essay I focus on commitment in marriage.

The term *commitment* has been used in many different ways in the scholarly literature. One important distinction that has been drawn in discussions of commitment is the distinction between (1) commitment as personal dedication and (2) commitment as conformity to external pressures, including the expectations of others. These two aspects of commitment are conceptually distinct and may vary with considerable independence. However, it may be that there are causal relations between the two. For example, it may be that the communication of one's personal dedication promotes expectations in others that bind one to the dedication one has communicated. Or it may be that external pressures, in some circumstances, produce personal dedication. Kanter (1972, pp. 66-67), in an exciting monograph dealing with commitment in nineteenth-century American communes, has chosen to define commitment as the conjunction of both personal dedication and external pressures. I prefer, however, to keep dedication and pressures separate, in part to facilitate theorizing and research on the relation between personal dedication and external pressure. For this essay, then, I prefer to define commitment as *an avowed or inferred intent of a person to*

Work on this paper was supported by the University of Minnesota Agricultural Experiment Station. I am indebted to Richard O. Bell, Michael R. Cunningham, David Olson, and Sandra L. Titus for stimulation in the preparation of this paper.

maintain a relationship. The verb *commit* refers in this essay to the process of moving individuals into a state of greater commitment than previously.

Commitment, as I conceive of it, can vary in strength, depending on how long-term it is (cf. Johnson, 1973). Thus, commitment could vary in strength from commitment to spend a moment together to commitment to spend a lifetime together. However, there seems to me to be more to commitment than variation in its time span. Commitment could be hedged by more or less conscious qualifications—for example, that alter continue to be accepting, attractive, and sexually interesting and ego continue to have the same values, preferences, and needs. In addition, commitments of equal strength within a given context could be different in resistance to changes in context—for example, change in availability of relationships with attractive others, change in what is the culturally ideal spouse, or change in the amount of time work obligations keep the couple apart. Hence, sophisticated operational definitions of commitment may have to sample commitment across situations.

Operational definitions of commitment as I conceptualize it could include avowed commitment and a number of indirect indicators—fantasies and plans of divorce, planning ahead as though the relationship is permanent, and tolerance of characteristics of one's spouse that many might find objectionable (e.g., a skin disease, moodiness, uncleanliness).

A difficulty in measuring commitment is that people may score artificially high as a result of situational pressures. The researcher must be sensitive to these situational pressures in the measurement situation and minimize them—for example, by assessing spouses in isolation from each other and by using disguised and indirect measurement techniques as well as self-reports by the people studied (cf. Olson, chap. 6, below).

I would not assume that a person is fully committed to a spouse simply because the two are married, nor do I believe that commitment as I define it is often at its maximum when a couple decides to marry. Rather, I believe that individuals vary quite a bit in the degree of commitment sufficient to get them into marriage. Frequently the commitment sufficient to get people into marriage may actually be rather weak. Of course, one's commitment or one's capacity for it may grow. People committed at or near their own capacity at the onset of marriage may grow both in capacity for commitment and in commitment itself as they acquire experience in marital and other relations, and as they free themselves from youthful idealism, insecurity, and self-deception.

In my current thinking, commitment is different from and perhaps even independent of love, attraction, intimacy, the quality of communication in a relationship, and marital satisfaction. If familiarity with the marriages of their kin, friends, and neighbors has not convinced scholars that marriages can be both unhappy and stable, the work of Cuber and Harroff (1965) and of Levinger (1965) may have. Any approach to marriage stability must work with the assumption that sources of happiness are at least moderately independent of sources of stability.

High commitment does not necessarily require an exclusive relationship, one without competing strong commitments; however, if either person in a couple defines high commitment as requiring exclusivity, then if either has strong competing ties high mutual commitment is likely to be absent. Consequently, in some couples but not in others strong friendships or strong ties with kin may be associated with weakened commitment. For people who do not define high commitment as involving a singular relationship, there may even be a positive association between high marital commitment and high commitment to other relationships. This could arise from individual differences in preference for relationships involving strong commitment or in the ability to sustain a high commitment (e.g., through tolerance, the ability to reward others, the ability to accommodate to changes in others, or stability of residence).

Paine's (1970) useful discussion of anthropological work on friendship leads me to believe that friendships may take some pressure off marital relationships. Thus, for couples who do not insist on singular commitment, strong marital commitment and strong commitment to other relationships may co-occur due to needs to escape from the constraints, tensions, and satiations of any single committed relationship.

I agree with Swensen (1973, p. 233) that relationships involving high commitment tend to be reciprocal, and with Blau (1964, pp. 84–85, 160) that exchange pressures tend to push couples toward symmetrical commitment. Nevertheless, there appear to be many marital relationships with asymmetrical commitment. To take cognizance of asymmetry, I prefer to write as though I am speaking of individuals rather than couples. That would free me to discuss the dynamics of relationships with commitment asymmetry. Marriages in many societies seem typically asymmetrical in the marital commitment of men and women, at least at some point in the domestic cycle. For some societies—e.g., the Kofyar (Netting, 1969)—women appear more likely than men to be low on commitment and to be the ones who initiate marriage termination. In our society, sexual stereotypes (e.g., the husband as the one who leaves when a marriage breaks up) have made it seem that women score higher than men on measures of marital commitment, though that remains to be established empirically and may not be true for some social categories. Gender asymmetry in commitment may be related to gender differences in access to potential alternative relationships, to local demography that makes one sex scarcer than the other, and to the degree to which people of one sex are or perceive themselves to be reliant on the other for life's necessities (Rosenblatt & Cunningham, 1976). It is also possible that a couple can be, on some measures, symmetrical and high on commitment but not perceive things that way. For example, one spouse may define high commitment as requiring singular commitment while the other does not.

The Social Psychology of Commitment

Having laid a framework for conceptualizing commitment, I would like to discuss some aspects of the social psychology of commitment. My discussion focuses on applications of cognitive consistency theory, on frames of reference for reward levels, on relationship context, on a "habits analysis" of marriage, and on commitment testing.

Applications of Cognitive Consistency Theory My use of consistency theory is eclectic but is derived mainly from Brehm and Cohen (1962) and from the modifications suggested by Bem (e.g., 1972). Consistency theory suggests that dispositional strength and stability are greater the more public, effortful, and voluntary has been the acquisition and previous expression of the disposition. To generalize, I would hypothesize that commitment is greater when it is acquired publicly, effortfully, and voluntarily (cf. Kiesler, 1971; Rubin, 1973). Although current findings on cognitive consistency offer only partial support for such hypotheses, the theory seems a useful heuristic device. Below, consistency theory is used to illuminate marriage ceremonies, the effects of children on marriages, and problem marriages.

Marriage ceremonies In societies around the world it is common for first marriages to begin with substantial publicity and ceremony (Rosenblatt & Unangst, 1974). The ceremony often involves public commitment to the new relationships by the bride and groom and by their close kin, and often the ceremony requires effortful activity on the part of at least some of these people. The high frequency of occurrence of publicity and effort at marrying suggests that they are indeed of value. When we examine variations in magnitude of ceremonial expenditure, attendance, and duration, it is striking that ceremonies are more substantial where marriages have bigger implications in terms of property and alliance (Rosenblatt & Unangst, 1974). One interpretation of that correlation is that where a marriage is of great value people work harder to commit its principals to the marriage (cf. Rosenblatt, Fugita, & McDowell, 1969). I think it is exceedingly difficult to make cross-cultural comparisons of marital commitment or stability of marriage, because societies differ so much in how marriages are defined. But I would suppose that by any measures, marital commitment and stability, at least in the early weeks of marriage, are positively associated with ceremonial effort and publicity.

Societies vary considerably in how voluntarily a typical bride or groom enters a first marriage. Even though in societies in which marriages are typically arranged there may be an element of volition for the couple being married (Rosenblatt & Cozby, 1972), societies with little freedom of choice and seemingly stable first marriages should be studied further. Such societies seem to coerce marital stability at the onset of marriage, yet they may, over the long run, build a commitment that survives the decay of coercing processes. By studying commitment-building mechanisms where the bride and groom's initial volition is weak, we might better understand marital dynamics in societies such as ours, where there are normative requirements for strong commitment before the onset of marriage. The possible commitment-building experiences that may be more easily studied in societies with little freedom of choice of spouse include interactions with own children and habit factors, both of which are discussed below.

My intent here is to persuade readers to do research, not to persuade them that something is true. In the case of wedding (and other) ceremonies, it seems to me that considerable research is needed. Conceivably, with the cooperation of some people who have the right to perform marriages, one could find people who would volunteer to be randomly assigned to ceremonial treatments varying in publicity and effort, if not in volition (see Cunningham & Rosenblatt, 1975). Dependent measures of commitment could be made with varying time lags following the time at which people are informed of their treatment condition and following their actual receipt of the treatment.

Children and commitment   There is plenty of evidence from non-Western societies that children stabilize marriages (Rosenblatt et al., 1973; Rosenblatt & Skoogberg, 1974). The evidence from the United States and other Western societies is more ambiguous (Chester, 1971). Moreover, since couples cannot be randomly assigned to parenthood, alternative interpretations of any statistical association within the United States would be difficult. Nonetheless, it is interesting to speculate about the effects of children on the marital commitment of their parents.

First, there is the problem of what people are committed to. It may be that, once a couple has a child, we have to take into account their commitment to the child as well as their commitment to each other. As Schneider (1968) has suggested, in his fascinating but poorly documented work on American kinship, Americans do not perceive the parent-child relation to be terminable. Psychological divorce from a child is for Americans far more difficult than divorce from a spouse. This does not preclude a legal divorce of parents, but it may deter divorce between parents still maintaining relationships with a dependent child. To determine the degree of deterrence, one could study the effect of children on divorce in societies differing in adherence to the notion of terminability of parent-child relationship.

Applying my heuristic version of consistency theory, it seems to me that the child serves as an audience that augments commitment to something. What that does to a marriage would depend on what parents do in front of the child. In theory, at least, parents who stage high commitment interactions in front of their child, but avoid commitment-threatening actions, would become more committed to each other. Conversely, parents who express anticommitment feelings in front of their child would tend to become less committed. Of course there are parents who expose children to both kinds of interactions and other parents who expose their children to neither. It does seem worthwhile investigating child-audience effects. There might be a possibility of experimentation with couples in counseling, randomly assigning couples to behave in different ways in front of their children. It might also be possible to study natural variations in what children witness.

Problem marriages My use of consistency theory leads to hypotheses about marriages with difficulties. It seems to me that couples who have severe problems—problems getting along, problems resulting from illness, unemployment, alcoholism, and so on—might become very strongly committed to each other. In theory, once spouses have engaged in some extreme effort and voluntarily remained in the marriage they will have substantial dissonance or self-perception pressures operating to promote commitment. I do not say that having a problem itself increases commitment but that staying with a problem while feeling that one could leave the relationship produces high commitment.

It has often been noted that the marital relationship of a person with a serious psychological problem supports the problem (e.g., DuPont & Grunebaum, 1968). It is consistent with my analysis of commitment that a partner who remains with a spouse who has serious psychological problems could adapt to the difficult relationship in a way that helps to maintain the difficulty. The husband of a paranoid woman may, for example, increase his commitment as her paranoia increases by acting as though he accepts her delusions. This would make it easier for him to stay with her, but minimize the pressure on her to change and increase her resistance to attempts at therapeutic change.

Frames of Reference Exchange theorists (e.g., Thibaut & Kelley, 1959; Blau, 1964) assert that one evaluates one's current reward level by comparing it with feasible alternatives. It is likely, however, that a person who is highly committed less often compares his or her spouse with potential alternative spouses. This could be true because the investments made in the marital relationship are so great that few or no other people could be real alternatives. In a long-term relation, one shares with one's spouse many memories that no other person could provide, and one's pattern of living might be so tied to one's spouse's patterns that no other person could provide the same level of comfort. A long-term relationship provides a frame of reference for judging current experiences and one's current self (cf. Berger & Kellner, 1964). In addition, one's effort to build accommodations and to tolerate difficulties might be so great that one could be very reluctant to lose those investments or to make similar investments in a new relationship.

If, for reasons such as these, people with high marital commitment do not have feasible alternative spouses, they may be less confident in evaluating their spouse or their marriage. People who monitor alternatives have a frame of reference for evaluating what they have. A frame of reference enables stable, confident judgment. Hence, when people with high marital commitment are asked how happy they are in marriage or how satisfied they are with their spouse, the question may not be meaningful to them. Without a frame of reference they will be inclined to give unreliable, extreme, and unconfident responses. This measurement artifact may underlie the apparent fact that marital satisfaction decreases over at least part of the family life cycle (see Rollins & Cannon, 1974, for a recent discussion of the literature in this area).

Extramarital or premarital sexual affairs, one's friendships and fantasies may represent a serious monitoring of alternate relationships, but they might represent many other dispositions, including simple pleasure seeking. As samplings of alternative relationships, affairs, friendships, and fantasies are unlikely to be comparable to marriage relationships. One of the primary reasons they are crude samplings is that they do not represent behavior under conditions of high or escalating commitment. For example, couples cohabiting without substantial commitment to each other differ from married couples in developing less territoriality about the use of furniture and storage places in the house, but they are more likely to maintain places in which they can have privacy from each other (Rosenblatt & Budd, 1975). The development of territoriality seems to depend on a commitment to remain together, as does the dropping of places to use for apartness. Thus, in the absence of high commitment to another person, it seems hard to determine what marriage to that person would be like. A person who realizes that it is difficult to predict the future of a relationship in the absence of high commitment might be more reluctant to end her or his marriage, simply because it is difficult to know whether any alternative spouse would be better than the present one. There is, then, a special problem in a society in which marital norms are high commitment norms, and that is that one cannot easily sample beforehand what the relationship will be like. This, I believe, will produce a substantial divorce rate as long as normative pressure for high commitment marriages persists. People will not be able to evaluate well what a marital relationship will be like until they are actually married.

Further, if pressure increases in the United States for high commitment marriages, the divorce rate might go up instead of down, since premarital relationships will be an even poorer sample of what marriage with high commitment will be like.

Commitment and Relationship Context Symbolic interaction theory contains the concept of "definition of the situation," which is applicable to commitment in marriages. If people define their relationship as deserving high commitment, they are more likely to commit themselves to it highly. Marriage ceremonies help to define the relationship as one of high commitment. A couple's children, kin, and friends help to maintain the couple's commitment by defining the relationship as a committed one. If so, when children leave home or a couple moves far from kin and friends, perhaps even when they go away on a vacation, the relationship may be weakened by the loss of such definitional input. The issue is complex, however, since definitions of a relationship as committed can lead to couple behavior that actually produces the commitment; conversely, committed behavior by a couple may itself bring forth the definition of the relationship provided by others. Although definitional pressures need not be maintained to keep a commitment level up in a couple with inherent high commitment, perhaps the pressures need to be maintained in relationships with inherent sources of instability.

As was suggested earlier, commitment may not be a static property, invariant across situations. Even if it appears stable across a range of counterpressures, many potential destabilizing forces will not have been sampled. A change in residence or a vacation may put a couple in contact with such destabilizing forces (Rosenblatt & Russell, 1975). For example, high commitment may be maintained by a residential arrangement that allows substantial privacy, by a life routine with a low amount of intimate interaction, and by employment arrangements or social obligations that keep a couple apart for 90 per cent of their waking hours. It may only be on a vacation, or when residence or job is changed, that the function of these maintenance conditions becomes clear. Hence, I would expect vacations and other changes in location and daily routines to lead some of the time to marital separations, the onset of affairs, or the seeking of marital counseling.

Another definitional factor in commitment is the spouses' joint construction of their current and past reality (Berger & Kellner, 1964).

Shared ways of understanding reality probably help to stabilize a relationship. Further, the more they have selected and distorted their agreed-upon reality, the more committed may the spouses be to the relationship.

Habits   In any long-term relationship, no matter how dreadful and unrewarding, some habitual patterns of interaction become part of one's life. The loss of such patterns is one reason the death of a spouse is so upsetting (Rosenblatt, Walsh, & Jackson, 1976); such a loss even leads to upset when a person divorces voluntarily (Waller, 1967). These patterns are in part associated with familiar environment. Hence, some of the pain and difficulty of disrupted patterns at the loss of a spouse may be reduced by a reduction in cues to the old relationship (Rosenblatt, Walsh, & Jackson, 1976). This suggests that commitment to a relationship increases with the buildup of habitual patterns of interaction. The more a couple has acquired interlocking patterns of living, the more committed the two spouses will be to their relationship. In addition, changes in situational cues and in patterns of living (if, for example, a couple moves, children leave home, or close friends or kin move) can be expected to reduce this commitment.

Commitment Testing   One phenomenon that I think occurs in marriage, particularly in early marriage and at life-cycle crises, can be called "commitment testing." This may consist of questioning the spouse directly about commitment, asking for favors, or being difficult in ways that allow the assessment of the spouse's reaction. For example, a wife's food cravings in pregnancy (Obeyesekere, 1963) can be interpreted as commitment tests designed so that the husband will come through, thereby convincing both spouses that their commitment is high. Cravings often seem to be for things that are difficult to get. That makes sense from a consistency-theory analysis of commitment; a husband's efforts will not only demonstrate his commitment but also increase it. It is appropriate that commitment should be increased before the birth of a child, since a stronger dedication to the marriage will be useful given the stress that children place on it (Rosenblatt, 1974).

Commitment changes probably occur relatively often at life crises or at ceremonial events requiring some expression of commitment. Perhaps if a spouse is unsure about commitment—for example, because circumstances have changed or there are new stresses on the relationship—he or she might then initiate a commitment test. How people do this has yet to be studied systematically. My bet is that people bias such tests so that the outcome will tend to be what they want. One can choose to make a request of spouse that is easy to grant. There is, moreover, another reason for making requests easy to grant. One might want to escape blame if the request is not granted and if commitment is thereby reduced.

Gains and Costs of High Commitment

One obvious gain from making a high commitment seems to be freedom from having to make decisions. Once one is dedicated to a relationship, the issue of whether it should be continued, the monitoring of alternative possibilities, or questions about how much one can take root in the relationship will no longer be present. This saves energy and allows time for other things. (I think the notion that all Americans are on the marriage market is interesting but wrong.) Of course, for some people the freedom from considering such decisions is a loss. Being so invested in a relationship that adulterous fantasies are no longer present or interesting is a real loss for some; being uninterested in developing lust for opposite-sex acquaintances may eliminate the pleasures of flirtatious interaction (Cozby & Rosenblatt, 1972).

Losses that derive from a marital commitment include an increment in agony if the relationship is ended—say, through death of spouse. Commitment also leads people to tolerate or maintain undesirable things in a relationship. Firm commitment might, as Blau (1964) or Thibaut and Kelley (1959) have suggested, make it impossible to use threats of withdrawal of commitment to influence one's spouse. Losing that threat may feel to some people like a deprivation. In addition, interpersonal insecurity can, for some people, lead to self-evaluation and discussions that would make them more attuned to problems in the marriage; highly committed relationships may, for some people, lack this self-evaluation and discussion. For such people, high commitment may lead to the tolerance of marital problems that might otherwise be dealt with constructively.

High commitment leads to laying down of roots. One is more likely to buy a house, to establish daily routines, to divide up some of the places of the dwelling for use by one or the other spouse but not both, to get into comfortable ruts regarding entertainment, visiting patterns, and self-presentation. All this may be comfortable, save time, and minimize friction. However, problems may arise if satiation occurs or situations and people change. Marriages with high commitment may lose some flexibility for accommodating to change. Nonetheless, one can argue that high-commitment relationships have more resiliency, in that people can get away with more alteration and experimentation since they feel secure with each other. But the situation may be complicated; commitment may be situationally specific. A relationship may be resilient when conditions are stable, but not when conditions change.

So:

Commitment in close social relationships is a topic that I think is of crucial importance, yet an American emphasis on happiness, liking, and sexual attraction, coupled with the difficulty of laboratory manipulation of commitment, has encouraged little research on the topic. In this essay I have suggested a number of researchable questions concerning marital commitment. Perhaps the best way to conclude the essay is to list the projects I have touched on that seem to me to be most needed. There is overlap among the projects listed, but each differs in focus from all the others.

Conceptual and Methodological Projects

1. Validity studies for the development of commitment measures
2. The effect of situational pressures on response to commitment measures
3. Relationship of commitment to love, marital satisfaction, and other standard measures of heterosexual relationship

Projects on the Development and Maintenance of Commitment

4. Commitment at the onset of marriage versus later in marriage
5. The development of commitment capacity
6. Effects of friendships on marital commitment
7. Sources of gender asymmetry in commitment
8. Effect of variations in marital ceremonies on consequent commitment

9. Commitment building in societies with little freedom of choice of spouse

10. Commitment to marriage and beliefs about terminability of the parent-child relationship

11. Effects of a child audience on parental commitment

12. Commitment in problem marriages

13. Investments in long-term relationships

14. Marital commitment norms and divorce

15. Effects of changes in relationship context on commitment

16. Commitment testing

17. Commitment and the distortion in shared construction of reality

Projects on the Consequences of Commitment

18. Commitment, monitoring of alternative relationships, and the evaluation of one's own marriage

19. Time, friction, and tranquillity in marriages varying in commitment

References

Bem, D. J. Self-perception theory. In L. Berkowitz (Ed.), *Advances in experimental social psychology, 6*, 1–62. New York: Academic Press, 1972.

Berger, P., & Kellner, H. Marriage and the construction of reality. *Diogenes*, 1964, *46*, 1–24.

Blau, P. M. *Exchange and power in social life.* New York: Wiley, 1964.

Brehm, J. W., & Cohen, A. R. *Explorations in cognitive dissonance.* New York: Wiley, 1962.

Chester, R. The duration of marriage to divorce. *British Journal of Sociology*, 1971, *22*, 172–182.

Cozby, P. C., & Rosenblatt, P. C. Flirting, *Sexual Behavior*, 1972, *2*, no. 10, 10–16.

Cuber, J. F., & Harroff, P. B. *Sex and the significant Americans.* Baltimore: Penguin, 1965.

Cunningham, M. R., & Rosenblatt, P. C. The application of social psychological knowledge: Commitment theory and marriage ceremonies. Manuscript, University of Minnesota, 1975.

DuPont, R. L., Jr., & Grunebaum, H. Willing victims: The husbands of paranoid wives. *American Journal of Psychiatry*, 1968, *125*, 151–159.

Johnson, M. P. Commitment: A conceptual structure and empirical application. *Sociological Quarterly*, 1973, *14*, 395–406.

Kanter, R. M. *Commitment and community: Communes and utopias in sociological perspective.* Cambridge: Harvard University Press, 1972.

Kiesler, C. A. *The psychology of commitment.* New York: Academic Press, 1971.

Levinger, G. Marital cohesiveness and dissolution: An integrative review. *Journal of Marriage and the Family*, 1965, *27*, 19–28.

Netting, R. McC. Women's weapons: The politics of domesticity among the Kofyar. *American Anthropologist*, 1969, *71*, 1037–1046.

Obeyesekere, G. Pregnancy cravings (*Dola-Duka*) in relation to social structure and personality in a Sinhalese village. *American Anthropologist*, 1963, *65*, 323–342.

Paine, R. Anthropological approaches to friendship. *Humanitas*, 1970, *6*, 139–159.

Rollins, B. C., & Cannon, K. L. Marital satisfaction over the family life cycle: A re-evaluation. *Journal of Marriage and the Family*, 1974, *36*, 271–282.

Rosenblatt, P. C. Behavior in public places: Comparisons of couples accompanied and unaccompanied by children. *Journal of Marriage and the Family*, 1974, *36*, 750–755.

Rosenblatt, P. C., & Budd, L. G. Territoriality and privacy in married and unmarried cohabiting couples. *Journal of Social Psychology*, 1975, *97*, 67–76.

Rosenblatt, P. C., & Cozby, P. C. Courtship patterns associated with freedom of choice of spouse. *Journal of Marriage and the Family*, 1972, *34*, 689–695.

Rosenblatt, P. C., & Cunningham, M. R. Sex differences in cross-cultural perspective. In B. Lloyd & J. Archer (Eds.), *Exploring sex differences*, pp. 71–94. London: Academic Press, 1976.

Rosenblatt, P. C.; Fugita, S. S.; & McDowell, K. V. Wealth transfer and restrictions on sexual relations during betrothal. *Ethnology*, 1969, *8*, 319–328.

Rosenblatt, P. C.; Peterson, P.; Portner, J.; Cleveland, M.; Mykkanen, A.; Foster, R.; Holm, G.; Joel, B.; Reisch, H.; Kreuscher, C.; & Phillips, R. A cross-cultural study of responses to childlessness. *Behavioral Science Notes*, 1973, *8*, 221–231.

Rosenblatt, P. C., & Russell, M. G. The social psychology of potential problems in family vacation travel. *Family Coordinator*, 1975, *24*, 209–215.

Rosenblatt, P. C., & Skoogberg, E. L. Birth order in cross-cultural perspective. *Developmental Psychology*, 1974, *10*, 48–54.

Rosenblatt, P. C., & Unangst, D. Marriage ceremonies: An exploratory cross-cultural study. *Journal of Comparative Family Studies*, 1974, *5*, 41–56.

Rosenblatt, P. C.; Walsh, R. P.; & Jackson, D. A. Breaking ties with deceased spouse. In A. Bharati (Ed.), *The realm of the extra human*, vol. 2. Paris: Mouton, 1976.

Rubin, Z. *Liking and loving.* New York: Holt, Rinehart, & Winston, 1973.

Schneider, D. M. *American kinship: A cultural account.* Englewood Cliffs, N.J.: Prentice-Hall, 1968.

Swensen, C. H., Jr. *Introduction to interpersonal relations.* Glenview, Ill.: Scott, Foresman, 1973.

Thibaut, J. W., & Kelley, H. H. *The social psychology of groups.* New York: Wiley, 1959.

van Gennep, A. *The rites of passage* (1909). Trans. M. B. Vizedom & G. L. Caffee. Chicago: University of Chicago Press, 1960.

Waller, W. *The old love and the new* (1930). Reprint. Carbondale: Southern Illinois University Press, 1967.

5

An Application of Attribution Theory to Research Methodology for Close Relationships

HAROLD H. KELLEY

Attribution theory deals with processes by which a naive person infers another person's intention from his or her behavior, judges another's ability from his performance, estimates another's attitude from what he says, or draws conclusions about why the person himself feels the way he does. In each of these cases, there is an observed *event*—an action, a performance, a comment, a feeling or emotional state. And in each instance, there is a judgment about some *causal factor* behind that event. The event is attributed to some property internal to the person (e.g., an intention or an ability) or some factor external to the person (e.g., social pressure, an authoritative command, something he ingested). Attributions are made about others, and they are made about one's own actions, feelings, or outcomes. They are an important aspect of social perception and self-perception.

Attributions in Close Relationships   Attributions are important in close relationships. Highly interdependent persons often have occasion to wonder about the causes of events in their relationship—why their love life is not more satisfying, why their partner is so influenceable by his or her family, whether a hurtful act was intentional or accidental. In a close relationship, we often explain our own actions to our partner; we also often tell our partner why he or she acted in some particular way.

Different attributions are often made for the same behavior or event;

Preparation of this paper was facilitated by a grant from the National Science Foundation, GS-33069X. J. William Dorris's helpful comments and George Levinger's skillful editing are warmly acknowledged.

when these are made known, they can become the basis for conflict. For example, a husband may feel that his complaint about a dinner is justified by its poor quality, but his wife "explains" to him that his complaint merely reflects the "bad day" he had at work. The husband's provocation from her "mind-reading act" (as Lederer & Jackson, 1968, refer to it) can be understood by noting that it simultaneously denies the validity of his complaint, challenges his dependability as a judge of food, and implies he is overly vulnerable to the stress of daily life.

The communication of attribution is particularly important during interpersonal conflict. At a simple level, such communication includes direct labeling statements such as "you're stupid," "you have a mean streak in you," "you did that on purpose." At a more complex level, conflict comments frequently *imply* attributions by referring to the frequency of a problem behavior ("you always act like this") or to the occasions of its occurrence ("you'll do it for your friends but not for me").

That attributions are important themes in interpersonal conflict is implied by a number of theoretical views. Heider suggests that revenge is aimed to correct another's negative attributions to oneself: The other person's original "harmful act represents a belief that the return action attempts to refute" (1958, p. 267). As it escalates, conflict usually spreads beyond areas originally at issue. In other words, conflict events and outcomes are seen to have implications for other times and situations, regarding relationship issues (e.g., who defers to whom) and the partners' own personal properties. Social scientists have noted this in various ways: They have pointed out that, in an intimate pair, dissension over one issue may spread to other areas of interaction (Becker & Useem, 1942); or that "the key objective of the typical family conflict is the simultaneous damage to the other's identity while protecting or enhancing one's own" (Turner, 1970, p. 145). Furthermore, it has been noted how threats tend to enlarge the arena of conflict, how they change the meaning of yielding to the partner's request and thereby introduce issues of "face" or self-esteem (Deutsch, 1973).

The preceding comments suggest possible directions for an analysis of close relationships from the perspective of attribution theory. To date, very little attributional research has been conducted on close relationships. An example of such research is provided by Cunningham's (1976) study of inferences made about liking, attraction, and pairing from observations of interaction patterns. Later, we will note the results from an investigation of attributional conflict, reported by Orvis, Kelley, and Butler (1976).

Attribution Theory and Methodology   Research on close relationships consists of investigators' attributions—about the persons involved, the relationships themselves, and the causal dynamics of the interaction process. The scientific method, I believe, is only a refinement of the naive, lay person's attributional process. Consequently, an examination of the naive process will afford a useful perspective on research methodology. Proceeding on that belief, I will first present a brief summary of attribution theory; this will amplify on how persons make attributions for events in close relationships. The second part will consider how investigators of close relationships make attributions about them, and some of our problems in doing so.

Some Concepts from Attribution Theory

Views of the attribution process have been presented in a variety of sources (e.g., Heider, 1958; Jones & Davis, 1965; Kelley, 1967; Jones et al., 1972; Bem, 1972; and Shaver, 1975). The present statement emphasizes primarily my own views (given in more detail in Kelley, 1973) and those concepts most applicable to interpersonal relations.

Attribution to Person, Stimulus, or Circumstances: The Analysis of Variance Model   Most instances of attribution, perhaps all, can be assimilated to the idea of making inferences about the cause or causes of a given effect from the distribution of that effect in relation to possible causes for it. In some cases, the cause is inferred on the basis of an *observed* pattern of an effect's occurrences; in other cases, the inference seems based on an *assumed* pattern. Such observed and assumed patterns can be conceived in terms of orthogonal matrices of information, akin to data matrices in the analysis of variance.

For a wide range of attributional problems, the most important classes of possible causes are (P) Persons, (S) Stimuli (things or entities), and (C) Circumstances (times or situations). Whether a given event is attributed to one or another of these factors depends upon the distribution of instances of that event in the data matrix: $P x S x C$

(Kelley, 1973). Applied to social events, the *P* term refers to individuals as actors while the *S* term refers to individuals as stimuli or targets of action.

Person attribution   Consider this example, adapted from McArthur (1972). The given event (effect) is that "John criticized Edward's conduct," and subjects are asked what caused this event. Subjects receive the following pattern of data: (1) "Hardly anyone else criticized Edward's conduct." (2) "John also criticizes almost every other person's conduct." (3) "In the past, John has almost always criticized Edward's conduct." What then was the event's probable cause? Was it something about John (Person), something about Edward's conduct (Stimulus), something about the particular circumstances (Circumstances), or some combination of these factors? As the reader too may judge, a large proportion of subjects here make a "person attribution." The event reflects mostly on John; in some sense, it is caused by John. This is an example of an event that is low in consensus (occurring only for a given Person), low in distinctiveness (occurring for all of the given class of Stimuli), and high in consistency (occurring repeatedly on different occasions). In short, an event that is uniquely associated with a given Person tends to be attributed to that person.

Stimulus attribution   A different example (adapted from Frieze & Weiner, 1971) concerns the interpretation of Jim's being unable to repair the toaster for his wife. The data pattern for this event is that "Almost all other husbands also are unable to repair this toaster. Jim is able to repair most other electrical appliances. Jim has never been able to repair this particular toaster in the past." This pattern of high consensus, high distinctiveness, and high consistency suggests that Jim's failure is due to the *toaster*, the repair of which is obviously difficult. The fact that failure is associated uniquely with the toaster means that we have learned something about it rather than something about Jim.

Situation attribution   A third distribution involves low consensus, high distinctiveness, and low consistency. Imagine that Joan declines Peter's invitation to dance. Additionally, you hear that "Hardly anyone else declines Peter's invitations. Joan declines few other men's invitations to dance. Joan had never similarly declined Peter's invitations in the past." The explanation for this declination can be found neither in Joan (that she is generally prone to decline such invitations) nor in Peter (that his invitations tend to elicit declinations). Therefore, the cause must be the particular situation in which the aberrant declination occurred.

In short, a main point of attribution theory is that the layman attributes causation for an event to the condition (or conditions) most closely associated with its occurrence. Beyond the single-cause attributions described above, there may also be attributions to the joint action of two causes. For example, if Mary rarely insults other persons but consistently insults Joan, and Joan is rarely insulted by others, an attribution is made to both Mary *and* Joan. There's something about them as a pair that brings out the worst in Mary.

The Assembly of Information As the above examples show, attribution theory assumes that the person interprets an event within the context of information about the circumstances and frequency of its occurrence. A number of studies show that people are indeed able to assemble such an interpretative context from their observation of successive instances of a type of event (Valins, 1966; Harvey & Kelley, 1974; Cunningham, 1976). Such information assembly occurs, of course, in any successful discrimination learning experiment as the subject learns to associate a particular response with a particular stimulus configuration. Information need not be assembled accurately or efficiently. The process is often slow and is susceptible to bias.

Close relationships, too, are marked by such information assembly (scorekeeping, comparing instances, examining the distribution of events). This is suggested by comments one hears, particularly at times of conflict. Remarks implying a person (actor) attribution would include "You always treat me this way" (high consistency), "You are mean like this to all of us, even to the children" (low distinctiveness), and "No one else treats me like this" (low consensus). Remarks suggesting an entity (stimulus or target) attribution might be as follows: "You always make me feel like walking over you" (high consistency); "I don't feel that way about other women" (high distinctiveness); and "Everybody tends to take advantage of you" (high consensus). In addition to such *distribution* statements, concerning distributions of effects over actors, targets, and occasions, there are also *instance* statements that merely *imply* an event's distribution. Examples would be the following: "You did the same thing last week" (high consistency); "On that fishing trip, you were not yourself" (low consistency); "You were nice to *her* at the party last night, but not to me" (high distinctiveness); and "Harry remembered *their* wedding anniversary" (low consensus).

In the real-life assembly of information, a central problem pertains to the equivalence among different events. If I have many opportunities to observe Mary's behavior toward Joan and also toward other persons, along with other persons' behavior toward Joan, what events would I regard as equivalent to (similar to, having the same meaning as) Mary's insulting remark to Joan? Attribution theory suggests that I will interpret the particular remark in the context of the distribution of other *similar* events, but it does not tell me what remarks will be considered "similar." Differing definitions of similarity are a common point of conflict in interpersonal relationships. A husband's response to his wife's remark that "You were treating *her* just like you do me!" is likely to be a denial of the similarity of the actions. (His response also is likely to associate a good reason with the action: "I was just being nice. Aren't we supposed to be nice to people at these parties?")

One obvious aspect of similarity concerns the identities of actors and targets (entities). In studies of the kinds described above (McArthur, 1972; Orvis et al., 1975), information about consistency has greater effect on attributions than information about distinctiveness or consensus: In the interpretation of A's present action toward B, A's prior actions toward B are seen to be more relevant than either A's prior actions toward other targets or other persons' actions toward B. This finding is understandable in terms of different degrees of comparability between the focal event and the contextual information.

Causal Schemata: Preconceptions about Causes　　When given only part of the information, subjects tend to fill in the rest of a "good" person, stimulus, or circumstance pattern (Orvis et al., 1975). Knowing that there is high consensus in reaction to a given stimulus, judges tend to assume that there is also high distinctiveness and high consistency, in order to complete the stimulus-attribution pattern. Or, given low distinctiveness, they assume low consensus and high consistency, thereby completing the person-attribution pattern. Thus, as mentioned earlier, the attribution process seems not only to take account of the event's *observed* distribution but also to proceed on the basis of an *assumed* distribution.

Assumed patterns of cause-effect data may be labeled as causal schemata (Kelley, 1972). From his experience with a particular kind of cause and effect connection, the person often has an a priori conception (or stereotype) of how a given effect is distributed over a matrix of possible causes. Each person has a repertoire of such schemata. He assumes different patterns for different kinds of effects.

The notion of causal schemata is illustrated by an example adapted from Jones and Harris (1967). Imagine these two attributional problems: (1) When given the assignment in his political science class of writing an essay about some Latin American government, Bill wrote an essay highly favorable to Castro's Cuba. What is Bill's probable attitude toward Castro? (2) When given the assignment by his political science professor to describe the progress made under the Castro regime, Jack wrote an essay highly favorable to Castro's Cuba. What is Jack's probable attitude toward Castro? In each case, the subject is told about a given effect (the favorable essay) and the state of one cause (external pressure to write a favorable essay, absent in case 1 and present in case 2) and is asked to infer the state of a second cause (the student's internal attitude: favorable toward Castro or not?). This comparison results in a more favorable attitude attributed to Bill, who wrote the favorable essay in the absence of external pressure, than to Jack, who wrote it under such pressure. This example illustrates the *discounting* principle, which states that "the role of a given cause in producing a given effect is discounted if other plausible causes are also present" (Kelley, 1971, p. 8).

In the above example, the effect of one present cause (i.e., external pressure) was to render ambiguous the inference regarding the other cause. However, there are certain cases where the effect of an external cause is just the opposite. In these instances, the cause is *inhibitory* in the sense that it tends to operate against the occurrence of the specified effect. The clearest example is external social pressure *against* taking a certain action. In this situation, if the attributor knows that the effect occurred with the external inhibitory cause present, he can conclude unequivocally that the facilitative internal cause was strongly present. This has been referred to as the *augmentation* principle.

In close relationships, the discounting principle is manifested by the fact that you cannot ask for a particular interaction and then be satisfied that your partner's compliance reflects true interest. As Lederer and Jackson have put it, "one *cannot* compel a 'spontaneous' response" (1968, p. 221). The discounting principle is shown in the following kind of comment: "You pay attention to me only when I ask you to. I don't think you really care for me." The augmentation principle might appear in one of the following forms: "You go out of your way to hurt me," or "You did that even though you knew it would hurt me." A more positive version might be, "You shouldn't have gone to so much trouble to get this expensive gift for me, saving your money and all. It really means a lot to me."

The discounting and augmentation reasoning illustrates the multiple sufficient cause schema, which is the assumption that the particular effect occurs if any of several causal conditions prevails. This is only one of several kinds of causal schemata. Various effects evoke different schemata for their interpretation. For example, success in a very difficult task evokes a multiple necessary cause schema, it being assumed that both effort and ability are required for its occurrence (Kun & Weiner, 1973). An interpersonal example: a husband's extremely frequent exercise of authority in the family will be taken to indicate *both* his strong personal disposition to dominate *and* his wife's extreme passiveness. There is evidence that some social behaviors evoke schemata in which the effect is assumed to be associated exclusively with the actor (e.g., John's feeling very inferior to Mike, which is attributed to John). Other behaviors are associated exclusively with the target (e.g., Ruth's extreme admiration for Martha is attributed to Martha). Strong liking and love are probably treated as emergent effects, arising from a particular combination of causes (both persons involved) and not predictable from information about the effects either partner generates independently (Cunningham & Kelley, 1975).

The general importance of causal schemata is that *they provide a basis for generalization from single events* (Kelley, 1972). That, of course, is the core meaning of attribution: An interpretation is made of factors behind the observed event, and this interpretation then implies when that event is expected to recur. Thus, our imputation of a pro-Castro attitude to Bill implies our expectation of his similar favorable behavior under different conditions. Our attribution of inferiority feelings to John, because he feels very inferior to Mike, implies our expectation that John will feel similarly inferior in relation to many other persons. Bob's ecstatic love for Carol, seen as an emergent effect of their unique relationship, will be assumed to be limited to their relationship and not characteristic of Bob's feeling toward other young ladies or of other men's responses to Carol.

Attributional Biases and Illusions   Another probable consequence of causal schemata (though it is not fully documented) is that schemata influence the intake of relevant information. A given schema represents a special belief about causation. Such a belief affects the attention the person gives to additional information, the readiness with which he learns it, and the accuracy with which he remembers it.

It is likely that causal beliefs, once firmly established, persist in the face of considerable counterevidence. This is the clear implication, for example, of the Chapmans' fine work (1967, 1969) on judges' perceptions of covariation between clinical patients' problems (the causes) and their responses to projective materials (the effects). A priori beliefs about these covariations lead judges to see them when not present and interfere with seeing other unexpected problem-response covariations that are indeed present in the data.

In the Chapmans' studies, the a priori beliefs themselves are very interesting. One tendency is to see covariants involving a *similarity* between cause and effect (e.g., a male patient's homosexual tendencies are perceived to be a cause that results in his seeing figures that are part man and part woman). Another tendency reflects a different implicit personality theory, in which the effect is perceived to be related to the cause in a *compensatory* manner (e.g., a male patient's concern about his masculinity is believed to result in his seeing broad-shouldered, well-muscled figures).

The idea of attributional illusion has not been thoroughly developed, but it is probably important for understanding interaction in close relationships. Thus, there are illusions of external constraint when one attributes to the situation or to the partner consequences that are generated by one's own behavior. This is illustrated by a competitive person's tendency to overlook his own part in eliciting competitive behavior from his partners, and by his related belief that "everyone is competitive" to justify his own competitiveness (Kelley & Stahelski, 1970). An example in which both partners overlook their own casual roles is provided by Watzlawick, Beavin, and Jackson (1967, p. 56). The husband says, "I withdraw because you nag," while the wife retorts, "I nag because you withdraw." As those authors emphasize, these comments describe the two different one-way causal sequences that are extracted from what is actually a circular causal process; each person's actions are both an effect of the other's prior behavior and a cause of the other's subsequent behavior.

Various attributional illusions appear shared by members of close relationships. An illusion of freedom may affect them jointly as a pair. They may have a sense that as a pair they do things out of choice; an observer of many pairs, considering the evidence of interpair uniformity, would recognize those actions as strongly externally determined. Or, a heterosexual pair may share an illusion about their pair's uniqueness. If their sexual interaction is limited to each other and generates unique feelings and behaviors, they may experience these effects as caused by something very special about their particular relationship, and not to be found elsewhere.

Actor-Observer Discrepancies   Illusions are often revealed by the fact that an actor makes a different attribution for his behavior than does an observer of that same behavior. This is a very important topic in attribution theory. Jones and Nisbett (1971) have proposed a general tendency for actors to attribute their actions to situational factors but for observers to explain the same actions in terms of stable personal disposition. They suggested that actors and observers differ in the information available to them and in the salience of the information. The actor ordinarily recalls his prior behavior in similar and related circumstances; so he is likely to be keenly aware of how his present behavior is inconsistent with his past and is therefore unique to the present situation. Further, because he is actively coping with the present situation, its distinctive properties are highly salient. For these reasons, he has evidence that supports an external, situational attribution for his present actions. In contrast, the observer sees more how the actor's behavior departs from that of others in similar circumstances (including perhaps the observer's own reactions). If the observed behavior is seen to be different, its uniqueness can then be attributed to the actor. Nisbett and his colleagues (Nisbett et al., 1973; Storms, 1973) have found confirmation of such differences in the actor and observer perspectives.

Under certain circumstances, however, the reverse of the Jones and Nisbett hypothesis is likely to hold true; the actor will attribute his behavior more to himself than will an observer. Clearly this would be true in instances of covert influence, where *A* rigs the situation to elicit a certain behavior from *B*. Whenever the observer departs from a passive role and actively attempts to control the actor, the Jones and Nisbett generalization probably tends to break down. (Indeed, Jones and Nisbett present their hypothesis as an "actuarial proposition" to which there are many exceptions.) The important point is that different perspectives on an event afford different contexts for its interpretation. Attributional analysis calls attention to what these differences might be and how they affect our explanations.

We might think that in close relationships informational differences between actors and observers would be minimal. In general, this may be true. However, even here, there are important actor-observer differences. In a recent study (Orvis, Kelley, & Butler, 1976), it was found that young couples can readily think of instances when the two of them give different explanations for the same behavior. The behaviors for which this is true are overwhelmingly ones disliked by the partner of the person enacting the behavior. Consistent with the Jones and Nisbett hypothesis, the actor typically explains the behavior in terms of external, temporary causes (e.g., circumstances, influence of other people, own physical state), but actors also frequently give justifying reasons such as concern for the partner and the inherent desirability of the activity. The partner's explanations are predominantly in terms of stable characteristics of the actor (e.g., laziness, weakness, bad character). These results bear not only on the question of actor-observer discrepancies but also, of course, on the use of attributional statements in dealing with events that are potentially disruptive of the close relationship.

Recapitulation We have shown how the attributional viewpoint describes the information that naive individuals use to make causal attributions, and the kinds of attributions they make for different events or patterns of information. Our analysis suggests something about the explanations people give for events in their close relationships—whether they will attribute the events to a given individual, to their relationship itself, or to situational factors. It also suggests the form of attributional comments, as a person communicates his casual inferences and the evidence on which he bases them. It is appropriate, therefore, to make an attributionally based content analysis of close interaction. In the present paper, however, we shall now turn our attention to how we, as investigators, make attributions about close relationships.

The Investigation of Close Relationships

Scientific versus Naive Attribution Processes   The investigation of a close relationship consists of the investigator's making attributions—about the individual members, about the relationship itself, and about the causes for events observed to occur there. Scientific research methodology is the layman's attribution process systematized, so as to reduce biases in attribution. As I have argued previously, "there are only a limited number of ways of making sense out of the available data about the world. . . . scientific procedures are merely refined and explicit versions of methods upon which the common man also comes to rely" (Kelley, 1972, p. 21). In that paper, I suggested that if there is such a continuity between scientific and everyday procedures, it is proper to draw upon the more explicit procedures for insights into the more implicit ones. Here the opposite tack is taken, scientific procedures being examined in the light of knowledge about the layman's attributional processes.

The connection between research method and naive attribution is fairly obvious. The essence of scientific method is careful attention to information from the external world. The procedures of science are designed to collect such information with minimal distortion, to permit its complete recording and retention, and to enable its assembly for the purpose of detecting underlying patterns. Scientists try to minimize the influence of their a priori beliefs (causal schemata) on processing such information.

The attributional criteria of consistency, distinctiveness, and consensus for evaluating the interpretation of one's knowledge have clear parallels in scientific method. *Consistency over time* corresponds to the evaluation of a measure's accuracy by ascertaining its test-retest reliability. *Consistency over different modalities* corresponds to the scientific criterion of consistency among multiple measures, their collective validity being established convergently. *Distinctiveness* (e.g., that I must react distinctively to an object if I am to feel that I know its properties) corresponds to a measure's discriminative power—its ability to differentiate among a number of instances (persons, groups, etc.) supposed to differ along some dimension. *Consensus* appears most systematically in scientific practice when we test for agreement among coders' or observers' judgments. The consensus criterion is also fulfilled by agreement among different investigators in their results, conclusions, or interpretations. Interinvestigator agreement is most impressive when we can be sure of their independence (an assumption in attribution theory pointed out by Heider, 1958). We are most impressed when competing investigators of different persuasions converge on the same interpretation; this makes collusion or subtle influence improbable, and it indicates the strength of the external causes to which all are responding. Consensus also appears in complex ways in our relations with our respondents. This last point will be discussed below as it relates to research on close relationships.

The experimental method, with its control of causal factors (independent variables) and measurement of effects (dependent variables), pertains to natural attribution in a complex way. Of course, the lay attributor often conducts "experiments" in the sense of manipulating causal factors and observing their effects. He may deliberately introduce variations in order to aid in making a confident causal inference (as when the husband tests his wife's loyalty by leaving her in the company of an attractive male, or when the wife tests her husband's attentiveness by changing her appearance). Good experiments consist not only of careful manipulation but also of careful *design*—that is, the independent manipulation of several factors in order to separate their effects. Inhelder and Piaget's (1958) observations suggest that by early adolescence individuals typically are able to plan and interpret "experiments" for disentangling the interplay of multiple causal factors.

Some Methodological Warnings Suggested by Attribution Research The preceding comments have suggested parallels between scientific and naive attributional process. It is therefore possible to draw upon attribution research for warnings for the scientist. These findings highlight the importance of methodological safeguards and caution us against the assumption that, simply because we act as scientists, we are immune to attributional mistakes.

The research of Loren and Jean Chapman (1967, 1969), mentioned earlier, suggests that without safeguards scientifically trained persons are subject to the same biases as are naive persons. They found that clinically naive undergraduate students, when shown projective test protocols randomly paired with descriptions of patients' problems, tended to see certain connections between the test responses and the problems. For example, subjects saw a large head drawn on the Draw-A-

Person Test associated with worry about one's intelligence, even though this "effect" and this "cause" were not actually covariant. More importantly, the students tended to "rediscover" the very same relations between test responses and problems that trained clinical psychologists report in their practice (but for which careful studies have found no evidence).

The point is that without the aid of careful record keeping and systematic cross-tabulation even attributors with scientific training can be misled by their "plausible" causal beliefs into thinking that they are confirmed by the information they observe. In family research, as Riskin and Faunce (1972) suggest, where different types of families are being compared, it is important that interviewers, coders, and raters be unaware of the types under consideration and of the label of any given family. These authors note some gross violations of this safeguard that are common in family research.

One remarkable finding in the Chapman research is how widely shared are some of the erroneous beliefs, reflected both in the consensus among the undergraduate subjects and in their agreement with the clinicians' reports. There was some evidence that these common beliefs have a basis in "associative connections"—some problems tending to "call to mind" signs with which they were erroneously seen to covary. There is probably a strong tendency for attributors to assume a similarity or a figural correspondence between cause and effect. Furthermore, causes and effects standing in such simple figural relationships not only are seen as covariant when they are not so in fact, but their presence interferes with the detection of covariation between causes and effects that are not figurally associable.

The tendency to assume that effects bear a simple correspondence to their causes probably takes its toll early in the reasearch process, limiting even the formulation of the investigator's initial set of causal hypotheses. How can an investigator break away from the tendency to limit his hypotheses to causes that appear "congruent" with effects? To avoid that hazard, need he rely on blind empiricism or serendipity? One alternative is "imaginative" theory construction, the imagining of complex rather than simple relations between effects and their causes. Where the layman looks only for pathological causes for such effects as divorce or the mentally ill family member, the theory-equipped scientist considers a broader set of plausible causes—including, for example, the possibility that perfectly well-intentioned or healthy persons can, through social interaction, produce such negative effects.

Earlier I described the Jones and Nisbett hypothesis, that observers tend to attribute an actor's behavior to his personal properties, whereas the actor himself attributes the same behavior to the situation. Scientific researchers too may attribute too much causality to individuals for the phenomena they observe. In family research, the emphasis on individuals as the primary unit of analysis has come under attack (e.g., Riskin & Faunce, 1972, pp. 395, 404-406). The scientist's bias toward persons as causes is understandable from an attributional viewpoint. Recall that Jones and Nisbett partially justify their hypothesis by the argument that the observer is more inclined to compare the actor with other actors and is highly sensitive to how the observed behavior differs from what other actors would do. The methodological paraphernalia for the study of close relationships, drawn primarily from psychology, tend to encourage precisely such comparisons among persons and the discrimination of individual differences. Devices for distinguishing types of relationships or variations in external circumstances (tasks, contexts, or patterns of interdependence) are far less well developed. Unfortunately, the scientist's very hypotheses are limited by the distinctions among causal factors permitted by his measurement tools.

The Interpretation of Subjects' Attributions   A recurring methodological question is what interpretation to place upon subjects' attributions. As we ourselves attempt to understand the events in a given relationship, its participants themselves are likely to make attributions for the same events. Knowing this, we are tempted to rely on them to help us explain the events we are trying to understand. Even if we wish to avoid such a dependence, it seems plausible to determine participants' attributions to compare them with our own. The methodological possibilities here are unique to social science. All sciences are concerned with causal explanation, but only in ours are the subjects of the investigation also concerned with and capable of causal explanation.

Methodological writings in the field of close relationships contain strong warnings against asking subjects for their attributions. Straus states the principle "that it is preferable to have the subject report specific acts or behaviors rather than generalizations about his behavior. The specific indicators are then used as a basis for generalization about his behavior *by the investigator*" (1964, p. 348). Straus argues that by asking the subject to make a generalization we sensitize him to its evaluative implications and motivate him to present himself in socially desirable terms.

There is no guarantee, of course, that as we elicit successive pieces of information the respondent will not be able to infer our objectives. From the point of view of attribution process, this raises some fascinating questions: When do research subjects begin to make attributions about the researcher's objectives? What information is necessary for them to uncover such purposes? Do our attempts at disguise lead them simply to make incorrect attributions, and are not their incorrect attributions as distorting of the research process as their correct ones?

Recognizing that the respondent may infer our research goals from our questions, Straus suggests methods to conceal these goals— interesting tactics when examined from an attributional viewpoint. One strategy of concealment is to ask questions bearing no superficial similarity to the property of interest. For example, certain scales on the MMPI have no simple resemblance to the attributes to which they are generalized.

A different strategy is to disguise the investigator's attributional intentions. Questions are posed not about the self or the relationship but merely about some external reality (how people whom you know feel; what families in general are like); the subject is given the impression that his responses are attributable to the external world rather than to himself or to his relationship. Unfortunately, the investigator's assumption in this technique, that the answers will in fact reveal something about the respondent, may not be entirely justified. Straus reports evidence from Getzels (1951) which suggests that, in responding to questions about what most people do or feel, subjects do *not* necessarily "project" (i.e., they do not permit their own properties to cause the response). Often, subjects take the investigator's ostensible purpose at face value and make a serious attempt to estimate popular behavior or opinion. The use of information tests as disguised self-report devices may also backfire; respondents can easily take the investigator's purpose as that of assessing not the external truth but their own ability to know that truth. As Straus notes, under these conditions respondents may become defensive about having their knowledge "tested."

A third procedure noted by Straus is to keep respondents so engrossed in some "absorbing situation" that they forget about the investigator and his attributional task. Presumably they will not have the opportunity to puzzle out the meaning of their behavior. This procedure is interesting, but unfortunately the attributional research to validate it has not been conducted. We have virtually no information about the circumstances under which people make attributions, when they are motivated to do so, or when other activities facilitate or interfere with the attribution process.

Questions of concealment or disguise aside, are we to take Straus seriously? Are we never to seek the attributions that our respondents make for their own behavior? Theoretically, the case is ambiguous. The respondents have had significant information that is unavailable except through them. This includes a distribution of the focal event over times and situations far beyond our view. They also have direct knowledge of their private purposes which they may or may not reveal to us. Furthermore, they are not contaminated with our own causal hypotheses.

On the other hand, we know little about respondents' retention and processing of their information. It is hardly reasonable to assume that they ask themselves "why?" about every event in their relationship. Thus, we are left with the question of how their attributional answers may be biased by being generated retrospectively, rather than spontaneously at the time of the events.

Although our respondents may not share our causal preconceptions, they undoubtedly have some of their own. They probably have simpler causal ideas than will be necessary for adequate scientific explanation. Respondents' explanations pertain most probably to either an Actor or a Target. They are less likely to pertain to the more complex Actor x Target or the Actor x Target x Situation attribution. And there is little doubt that respondents often present false but good reasons, rather than true but bad ones.

At present, we simply do not know when we should take subjects' attributions at face value and when we should discount them. A central dilemma in studying close relationships is that, as observers and outsiders, we find inadequate the available information but we feel uncomfortable about turning to the better informed attributors who are the inside participants. Yet it seems quite appropriate to give some weight to their attributions. At the least, we should elicit them in order to compare them with our own. And in view of the sharply different data available to them and to us (theirs being distributed over times and situations, and ours over persons and relationships), we should not be surprised to find discrepancies between our respective attributions.

One is forced to retreat to the cliché: More research is needed—more research on the participants' and on our own attribution processes. Also, more thought needs to be given to our own relationship with our subjects. For respondents are able not only to report their attributions but also to comment upon ours. Just as we can compare the two sets of attributions, so can they (though they may require a little coaching if we move to more complex levels of explanation). One might propose (as have Harré & Secord, 1972) a sort of "negotiation of attributions" between us and our subjects. This idea deserves further consideration elsewhere. In the present paper, we shall turn to one important research topic: the measurement of social power in close relationships.

The Attribution of Power in the Family The great interest in power relations in the family seems to stem from an assumption that causal factors under this rubric will explain important events such as family decisions. In this area there is considerable discrepancy between the actors' attributions and those made by investigators. Thus, family power assessment affords a good instance for examining attributional problems in research on close relationships. The present comments will rely heavily upon a pair of excellent studies by Olson (1969) and by Olson and Rabunsky (1972).

If one steps back from the details of the research on power, one is struck by its strong tendency toward "person attribution." Investigators of family power seem to seek the causes of events almost exclusively in persons or in the properties of persons. The research usually implies that one or the other member of the married couple must cause the final decision. Or perhaps both members determine the outcome, but merely as a result of their "relative influence" rather than any "interaction" or "emergent" effect. That the search for person-causes, rather than for more complex causes, may not be entirely warranted is acknowledged obliquely by comments such as "it is often difficult to know which person made the final decision, because of the give-and-take which occurs." (Elsewhere, however, it is suggested that the real person-cause for the outcome may be merely disguised: "the give-and-take that takes place in decision making usually disguises who actually made the final decision.")

There are many alternatives to a person-cause hypothesis for family decisions. For example, there is the clear possibility that the true causes for these events are to be found in interaction processes or in properties of the relationship rather than in its component members. Some consequences of making a different assumption are self-evident. One would no longer feel comfortable in asking a respondent to report simply on *who* will make (or who made) a given decision. If interaction processes are important, one would not be surprised to find that participants are able to predict the outcome of a decision process but not able to give useful causal explanations for its course. From experience with many such events, a person may be able to spin out a typical family scenario without having any particular insight into its causal dynamics.

Complete absence of insight is, however, the extreme possibility. My hunch is that the participants generally do make rather valid attributions about their joint decisions but that we have not yet learned to zero in on these attributions. One central question raised by the attributional perspective is how the instances from which they make their inferences correspond to those from which we make ours. In an observer's rating of a family's decision process, he is likely to give approximately equal weight to each part of their discussion. However, participants in the decision may recognize that a particular suggestion or comment played a crucial part in the decision and that others were trivial. Social processes are not smoothly cumulative in their development. They have critical points at which they suddenly change direction and speed. When we ourselves are participants in group discussions, we recognize these points; our recognition is sharpened by our acquaintance with the other discussants and their special interrelationships. Such acquaintance makes it plausible that a participant will make a veridical attribution of "influence" in a discussion that diverges from that of an outsider. In terms of our analysis of variance model of attribution, an observer often makes his inference from marginal totals ("he who talked the most exercised the most influence"). The insider, on the other hand, is often able to make an inference on the basis of a complex "interaction" effect: "given that we were discussing this particular topic and that X and Y had taken this position, what Z said determined the outcome."

One central point here concerns the investigator's own causal schema—the rule by which he infers "power" from certain "effects." Power is taken to mean something like causing the final decision, and as noted above, it is usually assumed to be a personal property. Thus, the attribution of power requires detecting instances where one or the other person can be inferred to be responsible for the final decision. Such instances exist when, before the discussion, the two persons have opposing preferences. Then, the decision itself can be compared with these opposing prediscussion preferences and is credited to the person to whose initial preference it conforms. In other words, the investigator assumes that the person whose initial preference more closely matches the final decision influenced the other to change toward him.

This attributional rule seems utterly reasonable. It would go unquestioned, were it not frequently inconsistent with the participants' own accounts of who made the decision. Although participants' attributions do not necessarily merit greater credence than the observer's, the discrepancy leads one to examine this rule closely. Note first that it is a correspondence rule of the type that the Chapmans' research warns us against. The cause of the decision is assumed to be that initial preference which most closely resembles it—or rather, it is the *possessor* of the similar initial opinion who is responsible for the decision. (The similarity bias plus the person bias?)

But how do initial preferences influence later decisions? Does the winning preference necessarily reflect something about its initial possessor's "power"? Or should one view the initial preferences or "positions" as packages of information, arguments, and evaluations? They are presented in the discussion for comparison and then, by virtue of their relative merits, one package is chosen. This would locate the cause of the decision in the properties of the "positions" rather than in the properties of the persons holding them. When we refocus the issue, we recognize certain simple alternatives to the conception of power as a property of the person. We also wonder what it might mean to a respondent to ask him, "Who will make the decision?" if the true locus of cause for the decision lies in properties of "positions." It is possible, for example, that this question elicits a commentary on the roles of the participants in selecting among the various initial positions and not on their possession of them.

To eliminate ambiguities about power, then, we must insist that the investigator gather information about the decision process itself. Mere information about initial individual preferences and final decisions will not suffice, because there are too many possible causal paths by which these may be associated. For these reasons, outside observation of a decision process may not be sufficient to identify its true causal relations. Such observation needs to be supplemented by careful inquiry into the participants' understanding. If the causal relations are complex (as they apparently are), then diverse data will be needed for their identification. Nor will the attributional problems be solved merely by specifying the investigator's "operational definition" of power as, say, the correspondence between initial preferences and group decision. This act of arbitrary definition gives the rest of us no reason to place more credence in the investigator's attribution of power than in the attributions made by his respondents.

An approach to social power that is more complex in its attributional assumptions is that of Raven and his colleagues (Raven, 1974; Raven, Centers, & Rodrigues, 1975). *Power* is defined as the potential influence an agent can exert on a target person, and *influence* as a change in the target that has its *origin* in the influencing agent. Although the latter definition seems to reflect a person-bias, further theoretical statements make it clear that the agent is assumed to play a variety of different causal roles and often to share the causal spotlight with other factors. Specifically, his power is assumed to have different "bases." In some cases, as for *reward, coercive,* and *expert* power, these bases are closely related to properties (or, at least, perceived properties) of the agent, such as his abilities and resources. However, the formulation also includes *information* power (which derives from properties of what are described above as "positions") and *legitimate* and *referent* power (which derive from properties of the agent-target relationship). There is clearly envisioned here a number of different causal sequences that eventuate in social influence, and these vary greatly in the manner and degree to which the change depends upon person attributes of the influence agent.

The Effect on the Relationship of the Investigator's Attribution Process   It is surprising to find little discussion of the possible effects of the research process upon the close relationship. Both methodological and ethical questions are involved inasmuch as the research procedures may affect the very data they yield and may change the course of the relationship in deleterious ways. As suggested above, the "why?" questions we ask and the information we elicit may themselves affect the participants' attributions. Participants may be stimulated to ask about events they have heretofore taken for granted. Even if we conceal our attributional goals, the information we elicit may direct attention to aspects of relationships that participants have not previously perceived. Even though participants have had access to such information, they may never have assembled it or considered our particular causal hypotheses. Our investigation may focus attention, then, on cause-effect connections that had previously escaped their notice.

Such new discovery can affect the definition of their relationship in various ways. For example, participants may learn that certain actions are occurring for inappropriate reasons. Or, they may discover that certain causal conditions are not resulting in the actions specified by their own norms. Highlighting such errors of commission and omission can stir up conflict between the participants. Attributional illusions that support the relationship may also be dispelled by our inquiry. The partners' shared beliefs that a negative action occurs for a good reason may be disproven if our queries about the instances of its occurrence suggest that its real cause is unacceptable.

The potential effects of our attributional operations are not to be taken lightly. While there is much to be said for a more interactive relation between investigator and participants (see earlier comments on "negotiating attributions"), such interaction increases these possibilities. The negotiation process could be considered a treatment or change process, particularly in view of the high credibility most investigators have with their subjects. Unfortunately, because few investigators have training in the clinical aspects of relationships, their potential for causing or exacerbating problems is probably greater than their skill in sensing and dealing with them. The ways in which research procedures parallel clinical treatment procedures must be carefully analyzed; methodologies that combine research with treatment should be more fully developed. Rubin and Mitchell (1976) have made an excellent start on the first task, but much remains to be done in creating the optimal blend of research and clinical practice.

Improving the Criterion of Collegial Consensus The most important criterion for the scientific attributor is consensus with his scientific colleagues. Any evaluation of a research method must consider how adequately it meets the criterion of peer consensus.

The consensus criterion is complex, because the scientist has several different audiences. These audiences include his scientific peers, his students, his colleagues in other disciplines, and the informed public. This multiplicity of audiences makes it possible for his work to receive consensual support when it is not entirely justified. He may find support from an unqualified audience, or he may get support from a moderately well-qualified audience but on spurious grounds (e.g., by virtue of authority over his students).

In the science of close relationships it is not easy to arrange for tests of collegial consensus. There appears to be considerable dissatisfaction with the comparability among studies and with the convergence among different investigators' attributions. Riskin and Faunce (1972) point to some of the conditions that seem to be the basis for this dissatisfaction: suggestively close but imperfect correspondence among investigators in their concepts and measures, use of samples that are difficult to compare, incomplete descriptions of methods, and poor control of contaminating variables—"There is poor comparability across studies, both in terms of the characteristics of populations to be compared and in terms of the great amount of variation in all aspects of methodology" (p. 404). There is a problem not merely of replicability but also of the degree of comparability across investigations necessary to provide a sense of their convergence or nonconvergence.

There is no easy solution to this problem of collegial consensus. Progress will require the cumulation of knowledge that is possible only through convergent generalization. Procedural standardization cannot be the answer until there is sufficient agreement on the most fruitful paradigms around which to crystallize the uniformity. In response to the same problem in experimental social psychology, my colleague, Gerald Shure, has suggested the desirability of introducing some standard measures to be used in all experiments. Such measures would be social psychological parallels to the standard demographic indices for characterizing a sample: for example, age, sex, education, or social class. Measures might include a standard characterization of a relationship or situation via, say, the dimensions of the Semantic Differential. The purpose is important—to enable each relationship or situation to be located in a social psychological space defined by standard coordinates and thus to be compared with relationships or situations employed in other investigations.

Riskin and Faunce propose another approach to collegial consensus that is worth our attention:

Several investigators would be invited to gather together to study a given family. . . . The entire group would observe a subject family interacting in response to some stimulus. . . . Each person would evaluate the family interaction in terms of his own particular theoretical framework and specific variables. . . . All of the observers would carefully study the others' reports. The several written reports would then serve as a basis for the group's discussing the family and attempting to clarify areas of overlap and differences, with special attention paid to explicating the reasons for the differences. [1972, p. 410]

One might wish to elaborate or modify Riskin and Faunce's proposal, for example, to employ a small number of comparisons, both among families and, within each family, among situations. The attribution process undoubtedly proceeds most expeditiously when each attributor can make comparative observations. And for reasons discussed earlier, we might wish to involve the family in the discussion in some manner. However, the essential idea is the important one: We need to invent procedures for facilitating consensus testing among different investigators.

Methodology versus Substantive Research   Paul Lazarsfeld is said to have expanded on an old saying in the following way: "If you can't do something, you teach; if you can't teach, you do research; and if you can't do research, you do methodology." Few of us would suppose that Lazarsfeld would seriously assign the subordinate role to methodology implied by this remark. However, there does seem to be a degree of denigration of methodology in some of the writings on family research. Referring to the measurement phase, Straus writes, "the problems involved are typically not as abstract and do not demand as high an order of intellectual ability as those involved in either research design (i.e., in deciding what to do) or research interpretation and writing (i.e., determining what the research shows)" (1964, p. 335). A more subtle belittling of methodology is provided by distinctions between methodological research, which should come first, and substantive research, which is implied to provide the real culmination of the effort.

I believe there is here a false distinction between method, on the one hand, and theory or substance on the other hand. We must recognize intimate links between methodology and substantive knowledge. Development of method always requires answers to certain substantive questions. An example of this point is provided by the present paper. Its central implication is that substantive research on attribution processes is necessary to developing a sound methodology for research on close relationships.

Every methodological problem in social psychology necessarily involves psychological and/or social psychological problems. Methodology should not be treated separately, but always in terms of the theories and data pertinent to its problems. "Methodological" research may be a necessary prelude to "substantive" research, but only in the sense that some substantive phenomena must be well understood before others can be intelligently investigated. The substantive knowledge necessary for a valid methodological strategy may not be in the focus of a particular investigator's interest, so he may hope that other scientists will provide the necessary information. Too often such information is lacking, so the investigator has to rely on his own hunches, only later to discover their inadequacy.

Conclusion

The present paper has been an argument that valid research on close relationships must be based on knowledge about our own and our subjects' attribution processes. Given that knowledge, we will no longer need to speculate about how to interpret their reports. We will be less puzzled and surprised by discrepancies between their inferences and ours. We will be able to improve upon our own attribution processes by reducing the distorting tendencies that characterize the layman's attributions. In short, I believe that empirical and theoretical progress in the attributional area will contribute to a sophisticated methodology for the study of close relationships. Drawing on current attributional research, this paper has pointed to possible problems in studying close relationships that derive from (1) an assumption of a simple similarity between causes and effects, (2) a tendency to seek explanations for complex events in terms of persons as causes, (3) a failure to analyze differences between the researcher's and the respondents' informational bases for their respective attributions, (4) a failure to take account of the effect of the researcher's information-gathering on the respondents' attributions, (5) an inadequate process for exchanging information in order to gain collegial consensus, and (6) a false distinction between substantive and methodological research.

References

Becker, H., & Useem, R. H. Sociological analysis of the dyad. *American Sociological Review*, 1942, 7, 13–26.

Bem, D. J. Self-perception theory. In L. Berkowitz (Ed.), *Advances in experimental social psychology*, vol. 6. New York: Academic Press, 1972.

Chapman, L. J., & Chapman, J. P. Genesis of popular but erroneous psychodiagnostic observations. *Journal of Abnormal Psychology*, 1967, 72, 193–204.

Chapman, L. J., & Chapman, J. P. Illusory correlation as an obstacle to the use of valid psychodiagnostic signs. *Journal of Abnormal Psychology*, 1969, 74, 271–280.

Cunningham, J. D. Boys and girls meet: Patterns of interaction and attribution in heterosexual attraction. *Journal of Personality and Social Psychology*, 1976, 34, 334–343.

Cunningham, J. D., & Kelley, H. H. Causal attributions for interpersonal events of varying magnitude. *Journal of Personality*, 1975, 43, 74–93.

Deutsch, M. The resolution of conflict. New Haven: Yale University Press, 1973.

Frieze, I., & Weiner, B. Cue utilization and attributional judgments for success and failure. *Journal of Personality*, 1971, 39, 591–605.

Getzels, J. W. The assessment of personality and prejudice by the method of paired direct and projective questions. Diss. Harvard University, 1951.

Harré, R., and Secord, P. F. *The explanation of social behavior.* London: Blackwell & Mott, 1972.

Harvey, J. H., & Kelley, H. H. Sense of own judgmental competence as a function of temporal pattern of stability-instability in judgment. *Journal of Personality and Social Psychology*, 1974, 29, 526–538.

Heider, F. *The psychology of interpersonal relations.* New York: Wiley, 1958.

Inhelder, B., & Piaget, J. *The growth of logical thinking from childhood to adolescence.* New York: Basic Books, 1958.

Jones, E. E., & Davis, K. E. From acts to dispositions. In L. Berkowitz (Ed.), *Advances in experimental social psychology*, vol. 2. New York: Academic Press, 1965.

Jones, E. E., & Harris, V. A. The attribution of attitudes. *Journal of Experimental Social Psychology*, 1967, 3, 1–24.

Jones, E. E.; Kanouse, D. E.; Kelley, H. H.; Nisbett, R. E.; Valins, S.; & Weiner, B. *Attribution: Perceiving the causes of behavior.* New York: General Learning Press, 1972.

Jones, E. E., & Nisbett, R. E. *The actor and the observer: Divergent perceptions of the causes of behavior.* Morristown, N.J.: General Learning Press, 1971.

Kelley, H. H. Attribution theory in social psychology. In D. Levine (Ed.), *Nebraska symposium on motivation, 1967.* Lincoln: University of Nebraska Press, 1967.

Kelley, H. H. *Attribution in social interaction.* New York: General Learning Press, 1971.

Kelley, H. H. *Causal schemata and the attribution process.* New York: General Learning Press, 1972.

Kelley, H. H. The processes of causal attribution. *American Psychologist*, 1973, 28, 107–128.

Kelley, H. H., & Stahelski, A. J. Social interaction basis of cooperators' and competitors' beliefs about others. *Journal of Personality and Social Psychology*, 1970, *16*, 66–91.

Kun, A., & Weiner, B. Necessary versus sufficient causal schemata for success and failure. *Journal of Research in Personality*, 1973, *7*, 197–207.

Lederer, W. J., & Jackson, D. D. *The mirages of marriage.* New York: W. W. Norton, 1968.

McArthur, L. A. The how and what of why: Some determinants and consequences of causal attribution. *Journal of Personality and Social Psychology*, 1972, *22*, 171–193.

Nisbett, R. E.; Caputo, C.; Legant, P.; & Marecek, J. Behavior as seen by the actor and as seen by the observer. *Journal of Personality and Social Psychology*, 1973, *27*, 154–164.

Olson, D. H. The measurement of family power by self-report and behavioral methods. *Journal of Marriage and the Family*, 1969, *31*, 545–550.

Olson, D. H., & Rabunsky, C. Validity of four measures of family power. *Journal of Marriage and the Family*, 1972, *34*, 224–234.

Orvis, B. R.; Cunningham, J. D.; & Kelley, H. H. A closer examination of causal inference: The roles of consensus, distinctiveness, and consistency information. *Journal of Personality and Social Psychology*, 1975, *32*, 605–616.

Orvis, B. R.; Kelley, H. H.; & Butler, D. Attributional conflict in young couples. In J. H. Harvey, W. J. Ickes, & R. E. Kidd (Eds.), *New directions in attributional research.* Hillsdale, N.J.: Erlbaum Associates, 1976.

Raven, B. H. The comparative analysis of power and power preference. In J. R. Tedeschi (Ed.), *Power and influence,* pp. 172–198. New York: Aldine-Atherton, 1974.

Raven, B. H.; Centers, R.; & Rodrigues, A. The bases of conjugal power. In R. E. Cromwell & D. H. Olson (Eds.), *Power in families,* pp. 217–232. San Francisco: Sage & Halsted/Wiley, 1975.

Riskin, J., & Faunce, E. E. An evaluative review of family interaction research. *Family Process*, 1972, *11*, 365–455.

Rubin, Z., & Mitchell, C. Couples research as couples counseling: Some unintended effects of studying close relationships. *American Psychologist*, 1976, *31*, 17–25.

Shaver, K. G. *An introduction to attribution processes.* Cambridge, Mass.: Winthrop, 1975.

Storms, M. D. Videotape and the attribution process: Reversing actors' and observers' points of view, *Journal of Personality and Social Psychology*, 1973, *27*, 165–175.

Straus, M. A. Measuring families. In H. T. Christensen (Ed.), *Handbook of marriage and the family,* pp. 335–400. Chicago: Rand McNally, 1964.

Turner, R. H. *Family interaction.* New York: Wiley, 1970.

Valins, S. Cognitive effects of false heart-rate feedback. *Journal of Personality and Social Psychology*, 1966, *4*, 400–408.

Watzlawick, P.; Beavin, J. H.; & Jackson, D. D. *Pragmatics of human communication.* London: Faber & Faber, 1967.

6

Insiders' and Outsiders' Views of Relationships: Research Studies

DAVID H. OLSON

One question that confronts social scientists interested in the study of interpersonal relationships is whose definition of reality is the most important, the individuals involved in the relationship (the insiders) or those who externally observe those individuals (the outsiders). Researchers interested in studying interpersonal relationships have generally adopted either the insider's or outsider's perspective. Those from the tradition of family sociology have tended to focus on the insider's perspective, while social psychologists have concentrated more attention on the outsider's perspective. More specifically, family sociologists have tended to rely on one family member—an insider—to report on his/her perception of reality. An implicit assumption of this approach is that the person reporting, usually the wife/mother, is providing information that is congruent with the other family members. This has not only led to the profession being labeled as "wives' family sociology" (Safilios-Rothschild, 1969), but it also ignores the accumulating evidence that the "perceived reality" of individual family members can be greatly divergent (Olson & Cromwell, 1975). As Jessie Bernard (1972) has clearly demonstrated, there is "his" marriage and "her" marriage. Social psychologists, on the other hand, have tended to rely on ad hoc dyadic groupings which are systematically observed by outsiders—usually research assistants—in laboratory settings with contrived experimental situations. This has resulted in a social psychology of dyadic relationships between strangers as observed by outsiders.

A major thesis of this paper is that insiders can provide information about their "subjective reality," and outsiders can provide data on "objective reality," and both realities are important if we are to gain a comprehensive picture of interpersonal relationships. The development of theoretical ideas about intimate relationships demands that we pay attention to both subjective and objective realities. While self-report measures can provide information from the perspective of the participants themselves (insiders) and the observational method can provide information about the family by external observers (outsiders), neither one is sufficient. As Levinger (1963) pointed out: "Progress in both theoretical and empirical understanding of family relationships will be speeded through the use of a combination of research methods in the same study—specifically, direct behavioral observation, together with indirect report by family members of other respondents" (p. 357). Unfortunately, more than a decade later, few investigators have taken Levinger's advice seriously; instead, they have continued to rely on only one of these research perspectives and have rarely combined them in the same study.

Because so few studies have utilized both perspectives, little has been made of the value and limitations of each approach to studying interpersonal relationships. However, there has been discussion of these issues in the larger area of psychology, as evidenced by the controversy between the phenomenologists and behaviorists who have debated the significance of their respective approaches for describing, explaining, and predicting human behavior (Kuenzli, 1959; Wann, 1964). Watson's dictum to "bury subjective subject matter" was later countered by Snygg and Combs, who emphasized that *All behavior, without exception, is completely determined by and pertinent to the phenomenal field of the behaving organism* (1949, p. 15, their italics). According to Boring (1957), John Watson was not against accepting verbal report if it could be observed and verified. This type of data, which will later be described as behavioral self-report data, is just now coming into vogue with behaviorists. The controversy still continues unabated with some social psychologists debating the relationship between attitudes and behavior (Deutscher, 1973) and with family sociologists determining whether self-report or behavioral data more adequately describe power and other dynamics in families (Safilios-Rothschild, 1972).

The philosophical assumptions, concepts, and particularly the methods used by investigators focusing on the "subjective reality" of

interpersonal and family relationships are different from those who have
focused on the "objective reality" of relationships. Unfortunately,
researchers have often used only one perspective, rather than taking
advantage of using both perspectives. Social scientists for the most part
have, therefore, failed to realize that there are two frames of reference
for understanding human behavior, the insiders' and the outsiders'
perspectives. These are two mutually exclusive frames of reference, and
neither is sufficient alone, but together they can provide a more
comprehensive understanding of interpersonal dynamics. This position
was clearly stated years ago in 1941 by Snygg but has not been seriously
considered in subsequent research on relationships:

> For whatever purpose behavior is to be studied, it must be observed
> from one of two distinct points of view. It may be studied
> objectively, as by an outside observer; or it may be studied
> phenomenologically, from the point of view of the behaving
> organism itself. The facts derived from these two points of view are
> non-identical and are often completely contradictory. As seen by
> an outside observer, for instance, learning is a process of progressive
> change in the learner's response to a static situation. . . . Since the
> situation remains unchanged, improvement is ascribed to hypo-
> thetical changes within the learner. . . . From the phenomenologi-
> cal point of view, that is to say, from the point of view of the
> learner, the facts are quite different. The learner remains
> unchanged. It is his experience of the situation or task which
> changes. [In Kuenzli, 1959, pp. 5-6]

The purpose of this paper is, first, to describe the research methods
that have been used to assess insiders' and outsiders' frames of reference
and to document the extent to which each point of view is considered in
current research. Second, the paper will review some studies that have
compared the self-report and the behavioral methods to illustrate that
the insiders' and outsiders' perspectives are really two different domains.
Lastly, the value of combining self-report and behavioral measures will
be discussed in terms of both theoretical and methodological rigor. It
will be maintained that only through the appropriate use of *both*
subjective and objective data can we develop a more valid theory of
interpersonal dynamics.

Table 1   Four Types of Research Methods

Reporter's Frame	Type of Data	
of Reference	Subjective	Objective
Insider	Self-report methods	Behavioral self-report methods
Outsider	Observer subjective reports	Behavioral methods

Research Methods for Assessing Insiders' and Outsiders' Perspectives

Table 1 is an attempt to describe the different research methods that can provide various types of data from an insider's and an outsider's perspective. An *insider* is defined as a member of a relationship who is able to provide information on both his/her own feelings and behavior, and his/her perceptions of the other members'. An *outsider* is any other observer of interaction.

Although the reporter's frame of reference (insider *vs.* outsider) and the types of data (subjective *vs.* objective) are stated as dichotomies, they truly represent extremes of a continuum. Thus, the insider-outsider dimension can represent a variety of perspectives ranging along this continuum. A simplistic distinction would be one between an active participant in the relationship, a participant observer, and an external, nonparticipating observer. These different roles affect the reports given about the same situation. Even the most objective coding of concrete behavior done by an external observer is influenced by the observer's bias.

Table 1 indicates four different types of research methods. The two types of methods used most frequently are self-report and behavioral methods. *Self-report methods* rely on an insider to provide information about his/her perceptions of the self or others (subjective data). Self-report measures can be broken into those where the focus is on the self and those which focus on another person or on a relationship. The self-concept and personality scales would represent dimensions in which the individual describes himself. Marital satisfaction/happiness and role performance/expectations represent dimensions which deal with a relationship. Although the latter are relationship dimensions, it should be emphasized that they can only be assessed by intrapersonal measures, and each person in a given relationship might perceive these same dimensions very differently. Questionnaires, interviews, and standardized tests are the most common self-report measures used.

In contrast, *behavioral methods* provide objective data about concrete observable behavior as reported by outsiders. This often occurs in controlled experiments conducted in a laboratory setting. The most common practice is to have observers code actual interaction using some coding system, such as Bales's Interaction Process Analysis (1970). Interrater reliability is then computed to determine the degree of agreement between the coders. Objective scores are then calculated on each of the code categories for a given person.

A newly emerging method, just beginning to be more fully utilized, is the *behavioral self-report*. This method bridges the gap between self-report and observational data. It is self-reported data, not of a subject's feelings, but of his own overt behavior. It is "objective" in that the same behavior can be observed and the scores can be verified by an outside observer. The behavioral self-report method has been used most extensively in behavior modification studies with individuals and families, but it could also be useful for research on concepts relevant to interpersonal dynamics.

The fourth method is the *observer subjective report*, which provides subjective data from the observer's (outsider's) perspective. This approach to studying relationships has been used primarily by therapists making clinical assessments and in anthropological studies of families in other cultures. Although behavior of individuals is observed, only subjective evaluations and descriptions are made, and objective scores on specific variables are not obtained as with behavioral methods.

One factor affecting the type of methods that a researcher can use is the role the subject plays in the research situation. There are basically four roles that a subject can play—participant, participant as observer, observer as participant, and external observer. The purest example of an insider is the participant role, and the purest example of an outsider is the external observer role. Both the participant as observer and the observer as participant reflect dual roles that are more apt to influence both the degree of bias and the variety of data that they can provide.

If a person is used only as a participant—an insider—then the researcher can use only self-report or behavioral self-report methods (table 1). At the opposite extreme, if an external observer—an outsider—is used, the researcher can only rely on observer (subjective) reports or behavioral methods. Although the roles of participant as observer or observer as participant allow one to use any of the four research methods (table 1), this potential advantage is limited by the degree of contamination caused by the mixed roles. The important point is that the researcher should be very clear what type of role the subject is playing and what type of method or methods will provide the most valid and useful data for a given study.

While this paper will focus on the value of using more than one of these four methodological approaches in a study, primary attention will be given to discussing and comparing the two most frequently used, that is, self-report and behavioral methods. This is primarily because the little methodological research that has been done has compared these two methods. This is not to say that the other two methods, observer subjective report and behavioral self-report, are of limited value. In fact, the converse seems true, but most investigators have not yet capitalized on the type of data that these methods can provide.

Researchers have tended to use *either* a self-report or a behavioral measure, rather than combining them in an integrative manner so that the same trait(s) could be tapped with two or more methods. This has seriously restricted the type and variety of theoretical concepts that can be measured and has reduced the methodological rigor of their studies. Later, some concepts and principles will be presented which require such multimethod approaches. Another consequence of using just one method is that the methodological rigor and validity of a study cannot be assessed. As Straus has emphasized, "Only if two or more methods are applied to quantification of the same property will it be possible to carry out really adequate validation studies" (1964, p. 392). Multitrait, multimethod studies, as proposed by Campbell and Fiske (1959) and conducted on the topic of family power by Cromwell, Klein, & Weiting (1975), can provide greater rigor to this content area.

Brief Review of Methodology
for Studying Intimate Relationships

In reviewing research studies of intimate relationships, primary attention will be given to the marriage and family literature. Two recent methodological surveys of this research literature reveal a heavy reliance on self-report methods used by themselves and a neglect of observational measures of marital and family behavior (Mogey, 1969; Ruano, Bruce, & McDermott, 1969).

Mogey (1969) sampled about 800 articles from over 8,000 articles published in the marriage and family area between 1957 and 1967. The self-report method (questionnaires or interviews) was used in about 45 percent of the studies published during each of those eleven years. Clinical observations declined from 15 percent in 1957 to 9 percent in 1967, but participant or controlled observation increased from 2.6 percent in 1957 to 13.9 percent in 1967.

A more recent survey of 600 marriage and family articles published between 1962 and 1968 in twelve relevant American journals was done by Ruano et al. (1969). They found also that the most popular method by far of data collection was self-report (65 percent); the questionnaire was used in 33.4 percent of these studies, followed by the interview (20 percent) or the two methods used in combination (9 percent). Secondary sources, such as census records, were used in 17.3 percent of the studies. Direct observational studies only accounted for 4.7 percent of the studies done during that period. In only 5.8 percent of the studies were self-report and behavioral methods used in the same study, and perhaps only a small portion of these had data from both methods on the same variables.

While marriage and family researchers have only recently begun to employ observational methods, social psychologists have relied more heavily on these methods, placing less emphasis on traditional self-report measures. Although social psychologists have tended to limit their investigation of interpersonal dynamics to ad hoc groups, they have developed more rigorous observational methodology that can be readily applied to studying behavior in more intimate relationships, namely, marriage and the family. Combining experimental-observational methods from social psychology with the recently emerging observational methods in the marriage and family field (Winter & Ferreira, 1969; Riskin & Faunce, 1972) could improve methodology for investigating interpersonal relationships.

In addition to the concern about the research methods per se, there is also an amazing lack of congruence between the conceptual unit and the subject unit actually sampled in research. The discrepancy becomes most apparent when self-report methods are used because behavioral measures require direct involvement of more of the relevant individuals. Reviewing the number of family members included in research studies,

Ruano et al. (1969) found that only one family member was involved in most studies (38.7 percent), with dyads used in about 33 percent of the studies, and total families in only 13.3 percent of the studies. When only one individual reported about the marital or family unit, it was usually the college student (53 percent) or the wife/mother (33 percent) but rarely the husband/father (3 percent). Unfortunately, both college students and wives have been chosen for the same reason, namely, their availability, and not because they are conceptually the most necessary or methodologically the most able to provide reliable or valid information.

Self-Report versus Behavioral Methods: A Methodological Review

The question of whether to use *either* a self-report or a behavioral method in research with couples and families is unfortunate, for it focuses attention on the advantages and limitations of each approach without shedding any light on the advantages of using both in the same study. As mentioned earlier, most studies of marriage or family relationships have used some form of self-report. Not until both self-report and behavioral methods began to be used together did investigators become aware of the different results provided by each method. This belated discovery produced some discussion regarding which approach was the most valid (Olson & Rabunsky, 1972).

The topic in family sociology which generated the most research and controversy in this regard is the study of marital and family power. This section will review some major studies using both methods in this area and indicate the degree of differences between them. A more complete discussion of advantages and limitations of self-report and behavioral methods of family power is reported elsewhere (Safilios-Rothschild, 1970; Olson & Rabunsky, 1972; Olson & Cromwell, 1975).

A pioneering study, which was a major stimulus for comparisons of self-report versus behavioral measures of family power, was done by Kenkel (1963). He investigated the relationship between a self-report measure of expected influence and a behavioral measure of actual influence derived from joint family discussions. Kenkel used a questionnaire to measure expected influence by having individuals indicate who would have the most influence in deciding how they would spend a $300 gift. Actual influence was assessed by examining which spouse actually made the decision after the couple jointly discussed their preferences. He found considerable difference between the measures of expected and actual influence. Whereas 48 percent of these spouses expected the husband to have the greatest influence, he actually had more influence in only 28 percent of these couples. While only 10 percent expected that the wife would have the greater influence, she actually did in 16 percent of the pairs. Forty-two percent of the spouses expected they would both have the same amount of influence (equalitarian pattern), and this sharing actually occurred in 56 percent of the families.

Kenkel (1963) also investigated the extent to which husbands and wives were aware of the actual roles they played in a family decision-making session. In his study, a comparison was made of "real roles" and "conceived roles" in family decision making. "Real roles" were those objectively described and recorded by an observer using Bales's (1970) Interaction Process Analysis (IPA). This measure represents the behavioral approach. The "conceived roles" consisted of the question-naire responses to the categories from Bales's IPA Scale. This measure is characteristic of the self-report approach. The questionnaire was given before and after the decision-making session. Comparing the responses of a husband and wife on the pre- and post-test questionnaire with the objective ratings that trained observers made of the decision-making session by that couple, very little agreement was found between questionnaire responses and observers' ratings. This difference indicated that the husbands and wives were not only unable to *predict* the amount of talking each would do during the session, how many ideas and suggestions each would contribute, or who would "keep things moving smoothly," but there was very little improvement in their ability to describe what happened after the session. Kenkel concluded that "These findings may indicate that the couples were unpracticed at even the relatively superficial degree of analysis necessary to recognize the part they play in a simple and structured interaction" (1963, p. 315).

Although couples are usually not called upon to describe the respective parts they play in a family interaction, this study by Kenkel indicates that they can neither predict nor recall family interaction patterns when this behavior is required. This study, therefore, strongly suggests that information about family decision making which is based on either prediction or recall data should not be accepted uncritically.

A second study which compared the self-report and behavioral approaches was done by Hill (1965). He was concerned with family authority patterns in three generations of families. He asked each spouse to indicate who made the final decision regarding six problems. These self-report responses were then categorized into one of the following three authority patterns: husband-centered, equalitarian, and wife-centered. The behavioral measure of family authority was obtained from a joint interview with both spouses. The interviewers recorded who did most of the talking, who exercised the most influence, and who seemed to have the last word. Hill stated that "We should note that the observers' reports identified much less equalitarianism and substantially more wife-centeredness in all three generations than the self-report" (1965, p. 127). In comparing the three generations of families on self-report and behavioral measures, 77 percent of the self-report responses fell into an equalitarian category, whereas only 39 percent of the observers' ratings fell into that category. Observers' ratings of the families reported considerably more wife-centered behavior (28 percent) than that perceived by the family members (7 percent). Observers' ratings also indicated more husband-centered behavior (33 percent) than was reported by the husband and wife themselves (16 percent). In other words, Hill's study demonstrated that there is considerable discrepancy between what is reported by couples about their behavior and what is observed.

Levinger (1963) used two behavioral measures and one self-report measure in order to determine the strengths and weaknesses of those three methods. In his study, thirty-one families were asked to complete ten family tasks and to complete Leary's Interpersonal Checklist. Two behavioral measures were obtained using Bales's Interaction Process Analysis and judges' ratings of the family's performance on the ten tasks. His self-report measure was based on the results from Leary's Checklist. Levinger reported that "Judges' ratings were obtained from the clinic sample of seven families, but these agreed almost perfectly with the observational (Bales's IPA) findings" (1963, p. 364). Although there was general agreement between the two behavioral measures, there was little agreement between these measures and the self-report measure. Levinger (1963) concluded that "The Checklist data corresponded only grossly with the observational data in *total group comparisons*" (1963, p. 364).

A study conducted by Bachove and Zubaly (1959) compared five different measures of dominance in nineteen families. They used four measures of dominance which represent the behavioral approach and one measure which can be characterized as a self-report measure. Two of the behavioral measures of dominance were taken from the coding of family interaction using Bales's Interaction Process Analysis. A third behavioral measure was a measure of power derived using Strodtbeck's scoring method. This measure is based on the number of suggestions made by an individual that are accepted by the family. The fourth behavioral measure of dominance was the interviewer's rating as to which spouse was dominant. The self-report measure was the Leary Interpersonal Checklist.

The findings of Bachove and Zubaly indicated little agreement between the self-report measure and the four behavioral measures of family dominance. In twelve of the nineteen families included in this study, one member was perceived as dominant by both self and spouse on Leary's Interpersonal Checklist (ICL). In these twelve cases, little relationship was found between the ICL and the Bales scores; there was agreement between Strodtbeck's power score and the ICL; and the greatest amount of agreement was found between the interviewer's ratings and the ICL. In ten of the twelve families, the interviewer's ratings agreed with the ICL regarding which family member was dominant. In concluding these comparisons, it should be pointed out that seven of the nineteen families in this study were not included because there was no agreement on the ICL regarding which spouse was dominant. Bachove and Zubaly concluded that "The comparison between findings about families' behavior and their perceptions showed that in a number of families the dominant person in the performance session was not perceived as dominant by others" (1959, p. 57). This study demonstrates a lack of congruence between self-report and behavioral measures of dominance.

More recently, this writer completed a methodological study of the correspondence between self-report and behavioral measures of power (Olson, 1969) and a related study of their comparative validity (Olson & Rabunsky, 1972). In these two studies, the various types of family power measures were obtained from a questionnaire administered to husbands and wives separately. Also, Strodtbeck's revealed difference technique (RDT) was used to generate items for the couple to discuss and resolve (behavioral measure). As in previous studies of family power, there was little correspondence between results from self-report and from behavioral measures. The validity study revealed that neither method was valid since neither related to the actual decisions these couples made.

Objective and Subjective Realities:
Reconsidering the Validity Issues

In conclusion, this review has indicated that in studies of family power dynamics there is a consistent difference between what is reported on questionnaires and what is observed when couples interact. Similar discrepancies between these two types of methods have also been found in studies dealing with family support (O'Dowd, 1973) and with other areas of family functioning (Weller & Luchterhand, 1969; McCord & McCord, 1961). The most typical reaction is to assume that the self-report is invalid and therefore should not be used. However, it is equally tenable that the behavior data are invalid. As R. K. Merton said in an article in 1940 when addressing a similar issue:

> The metaphysical assumption is tacitly introduced that in one sense or another overt behavior is "more real" than verbal behavior. This assumption is both unwarranted and scientifically meaningless. . . . In some situations, it may be discovered that overt behavior is a more reliable basis for drawing inferences about future behavior (overt and verbal). In other situations, it may be found that verbal responses are a tolerably accurate guide to future behavior (overt and verbal). It should not be forgotten that overt actions may deceive; that they, just as "derivations" or "speech reactions" may be deliberately designed to disguise or to conceal private attitudes. . . .The a priori assumption that verbal responses are simply epiphenomenal is to be accorded no greater weight than . . . the assumption that words do not deceive nor actions lie. [Merton, in Deutscher, 1973, p. 30]

In a review of social psychology research comparing the association between attitudes and behavior, individual attitudes (self-report) were also found to differ from their behavior (Ehrlich, 1969). One interpretation of the attitude-behavior discrepancy is that attitudes are a poor predictor of behavior and are, therefore, invalid. A more tenable explanation is that these studies are tapping two different realities, the subjective realities of the subjects (i.e., attitudes) and the objective reality perceived by observers (i.e., behavior).

One tenable argument for the consistent differences between self-report and behavioral data is that the conceptual definitions used in comparing these two domains are confused or conflicting. In addition, the methods of measuring both domains may be imprecise or inconsistent. Also, the sampling of related material may not be adequately controlled. A detailed review of these issues regarding attitude-behavior research (Ehrlich, 1969; Deutscher, 1973) and family power (Olson & Cromwell, 1975) can be found elsewhere.

The thesis advanced in this paper is that it should be not only expected but assumed that there will generally be discrepancies between data from self-report and from behavior methods. As Deutscher has emphasized: "No matter what one's theoretical orientation may be, he has no reason to expect congruence between attitudes and actions and every reason to find discrepancies between them" (1966, p. 247). It is further hypothesized that the discrepancy occurs because these methods are tapping two different domains, the subjective and the objective realities. As Riley (1964) has said:

> Observation and questioning often give quite different results; but this occurs not because one method is necessarily more valid than the other, but because the two focus directly on different, though interrelated, sets of social system properties. . . . Observation focuses on the network of overt actions and reactions among group members—the objective properties of the system. Questioning deals with the subjective network of orientations and interpersonal relationships—the underlying ideas and feelings and perceptions of the members. . . . Yet the data obtained by questioning and observation differ only in their direct foci. Indirectly, they are inextricably bound together, because actions and orientation, though distinguishable types of properties, are interdependent aspects of the same system. [P. 996]

Further evidence that these two types of measures tap different aspects of reality is contained in studies using more than one self-report or behavioral measure. These studies have found consistent differences between the self-report and behavioral measures and have found high agreement within methods (Levinger, 1963; O'Dowd, 1973; Olson &

Rabunsky, 1972; Turk & Bell, 1972). For example, O'Dowd studied family supportiveness and found rather low and insignificant correlations between self-report measures and behavioral measures ($r = .26$) but high and significant correlations between the two self-report measures ($r = .77$) and between the two behavioral measures ($r = .67$).

The significant issue is not, therefore, that these methods provide discrepant data but how such discrepant data can be used to develop theoretical formulations.

Combining Various Methods: The Best of Both Worlds

Rather than arguing whether to select a self-report or a behavioral measure, serious consideration should be given to including two or more of the methods presented in table 1. Such an approach has potentials both theoretically and methodologically. The rest of the paper will describe how an integration of methods is not only helpful but often necessary for adequate measurement.

First, some theoretical concepts dealing with interpersonal relationships require both self-report and behavioral measures. While some concepts can be measured using only one type of research method, other concepts necessitate more than one approach. For example, only self-report methods can be used to measure certain dimensions related to the self (self-concept, attitudes, personality) or to assess descriptions of relationships with others (role expectations, marital satisfaction). Also, certain interaction processes can only be measured using behavioral methods. However, most interpersonal concepts can be more adequately understood if measured from a multimethod approach.

It is somewhat ironic that, although many researchers espouse an interest in marital and family dynamics, most actual studies rely almost exclusively on self-report. For example, one of the most frequently studied areas in the family field is "family decision making." However, most studies have relied on only one family member's report and have rarely observed actual families while making important life decisions.

A study that demonstrates the value of combining self-report and behavior data is a recent multimethod single-trait study by O'Dowd (1973). She was interested in the degree of supportiveness in families where there was an addicted adolescent in contrast to families where the adolescent was not addicted. All family members provided information on supportiveness using two self-report scales and interacted together in two situations (the SIMFAM game and a family meal), which provided the behavioral data on supportiveness. She found that addicted adolescents perceived the other family members giving significantly less support to them than did nonaddicted adolescents. All the addicted adolescents' family members, with the exception of the mother, reported they gave significantly less support than did family members of the nonaddicted adolescent. Behavioral data confirmed that the addicted adolescent actually received significantly less support from all family members.

By utilizing both self-report and behavioral methods, O'Dowd was able to demonstrate the significance of the supportiveness dimension and was also able to increase the validity of her findings. Furthermore, there was an additional benefit from this multimethod approach. Mothers of addicted adolescents perceived themselves as giving as much support as did mothers of the nonaddicted, but the addicted child did not perceive it and it was not observed during the interaction. In other words, it appears that mothers of the addicted were prone to distort their degree of supportiveness in a socially desirable direction in giving their self-reports. Had the investigator relied exclusively on the mothers' own perceptions, no differences would have been found between the two types of families, and an opposite conclusion would have been reached.

Another reason for using both self-report and behavioral methods in the same study is that it can help an investigator to clarify conflicting findings in the field. For example, in a study comparing self-report and behavioral measures of power (Olson, 1969), the expected differences between the two methods were noted. In order to discover whether the data varied systematically, Olson used Parsons's theory of role differentiation in the family. According to Parsons, husbands would tend to play the instrumental role of giving and making suggestions, whereas wives lean toward the expressive role of maintaining harmony in the family. Although our culture is subscribing increasingly to equalitarian ideals, it is still more acceptable for the husband to be more dominant than the wife. Thus, it was hypothesized that husbands' self-reports would overestimate their actual power and wives would tend to underestimate theirs. This hypothesis was supported. The study not only provides a rationale for part of the discrepancy between the two measures, but it also helps to clarify some conflicting findings in the literature.

An increasing number of theoretical questions can be investigated only if both types of methods are included. For example, how does cognition affect behavior and behavior affect cognitive processes? Is it possible for behavior to change without accompanying changes in cognition? Or can a person's attitudes and beliefs change without his behavior changing? Attribution theory (Kelley, 1967; Jones et al., 1971) can also be studied by assessing behavior and then ascertaining the causes that the individual attributes to that behavior.

Using a multimethod approach can help to clarify interpersonal dynamics and how they are perceived from different perspectives — participant, participant observer, and external observer. When both spouses are questioned in the same study, they usually report on their relationship differently (Olson & Rabunsky, 1972). This difference is magnified as one moves from factual information to interpersonal dynamics, as the difference among subjective realities increases (Larson, 1974). And, if there are conflicting perceptions of reality when both individuals are describing the same relationship (both insiders), the complexities increase when outsiders' views are also considered.

How data from a subject's self-report, from participant observers, and from external observers' reports will give a more complete picture of interpersonal dynamics is shown in a recent study which evaluated a communication training program (Olson, Berlin & Moyer, 1975). These three perspectives are arranged along the insider-outsider dimension, with a subject's self-report representing the insider perspective, the external observers' the outsider perspective, and the participant observers' falling in between these two extremes. The training consisted of a four-week, eight-hour-per-day program, in which persons worked primarily in quads. Pre- and post-testing of skills were done by having trainees jointly discuss common communication problems. Their half-hour interaction was videotaped and later coded by external observers using a variety of scales (on speaker and listener skills, empathy, self-disclosure, etc.). Participants rated themselves immediately after each discussion and also rated (as participant observers) each of the other three members in their quad.

As expected, the pre-post changes varied considerably depending on whether scores were obtained from the participants, from the participant observers, or from the external observers. During pretesting, the participants' and participant observers' reports were rather similar in both the training and control group; but both sets of ratings differed significantly from the external observers' evaluations. Participants consistently gave more positive ratings to themselves and others in the quad than did the external observers.

At the time of the post-test in the training group, the three sets of ratings were much closer together, with those of the participant observers and the external observers the closest. The control group's post-test ratings did not change significantly from any of the three perspectives. One interpretation of this finding is that individuals were trained to become more aware of their own behavior and to be better observers of others. It also indicates that we can expect very different findings, depending on a rater's degree of insider or outsider perspective, namely, whether self, participant observer, or external observer.

Behavioral Self-Reports and Observer Reports: The Neglected Approaches

Most attention has here been focused on self-report and behavioral methods, but something should be said about the value of behavioral self-reports. Such reports usually refer to a subject's own behavior, but they can also refer to others with whom one interacts. Not only can this method bridge the gap between traditional self-report and behavioral methods, but it also has useful theoretical and clinical implications. For example, McFall (1970) found that when a subject monitors his own behavior he tends to change his behavior. When smokers monitored their own smoking, he found that they tended to reduce their smoking as a result of this monitoring process. For a researcher, this method may seem to be another source of reactivity (Webb et al., 1966), but for a behavior therapist, it is an additional therapeutic tool for reducing undesirable behavior. This method can also be of value in investigations of cognitive dissonance or of hypotheses that we infer our beliefs and attitudes from our behavior (e.g., Bem, 1972). While behavioral self-reports would provide information about how the person perceives his own behavior, attitudes could be assessed by a variety of self-report methods.

While observer reports have been the preferred method of ethnographers and also have been used by psychotherapists, this approach has seen only limited use outside those fields. Although these reports are biased through the glasses of the observer, and are criticized for providing only "soft" data, they often provide valuable starting points for theorizing. Such reports aid an investigator in selecting variables and developing important theoretical questions. This approach is most valuable at early stages of investigation. Once adequate observation is completed and relevant variables have been selected, then more empirical work can begin.

Unfortunately, much of what is published on interpersonal relationships indicates a lack of familiarity with the significant variables. As Sanford (1965) commented in discussing similar lacks elsewhere in psychology:

> you realize that the authors have never looked at human experience, they went straight from the textbook or journal to the laboratory, and thence into print and thence into the business of getting research grants. . . . psychological researchers do not know what goes on in human beings, and their work shows it. Not only is it dull . . . but it is often wrong. [P. 192]

The time is ripe for the use of observer-report methods to describe interpersonal relationships as they really occur in natural settings. These reports can help us focus on a wider range of relevant variables and questions than have been studied to date. Too little past research has dealt with meaningful questions of how relationships are developed, maintained, and improved, or how they change over time. Too much attention has been given to what Levinger (1974) calls unilateral awareness and surface contact, and too little to deeper relationships. Our challenge now is to broaden our perspectives as well as our methodologies.

Summary

This paper has discussed the methodology used in studies of interpersonal relationships, especially in marriage and family research. A research model was developed that utilized the reporter's frame of reference (insider *vs.* outsider) and the type of data (subjective *vs.* objective). This 2 x 2 model was employed to delineate four research methods which can be used to study interpersonal relationships: self-report methods, observer-report methods, behavioral self-report methods, and behavioral methods. While major consideration was given to self-report and behavioral methods, researchers were encouraged to expand their methodological repertoire. Rather than giving preference to either self-report or behavioral measures, this paper has emphasized the theoretical and methodological value of both types of measures in the same study. Such a combined approach was also advocated in a paper on pair relatedness by Levinger (1974), which describes types of individual and couple data that can be obtained through self-report and behavioral data.

Increasingly, our theoretical formulations demand data from both an insider's and outsider's frame of reference. In addition to including these two types of perspectives, it is hoped that researchers will see the value of using multimethod approaches. More serious consideration should be given to the advantages of multitrait, multimethod (Campbell & Fiske, 1959) research strategies to obtain data on the complex questions about interpersonal relationships.

References

Bachove, C., & Zubaly, B. M. An exploratory study of family interrelationships in a small sample of non-clinic families. Master's thesis, Bryn Mawr College, 1959.

Bales, R. F. *Personality and interpersonal behavior.* New York: Holt, Rinehart, & Winston, 1970.

Bem, D. J. Self-perception theory. In L. Berkowitz (Ed.), *Advances in experimental social psychology,* vol. 6. New York: Academic Press, 1972.

Bernard, J. *The future of marriage.* New York: World, 1972.

Boring, E. G. *A history of experimental psychology* (2nd ed.). New York: Appleton Century-Crofts, 1957.

Campbell, D. T., & Fiske, D. W. Convergent and discriminate validation by the multitrait, multi-method matrix. *Psychological Bulletin,* 1959, *56,* 81–105.

Cromwell, R. C.; Klein, D. M.; & Weiting, S. G. An evaluation of two methods of measuring family power by multi-trait, multi-method matrix analysis. In R. C. Cromwell & D. H. Olson (Eds.), *Power in families.* San Francisco: Sage & Halsted/Wiley, 1975.

Deutscher, I. Words and deeds: Social science and social policy. *Social Problems,* 1966, *13,* 235–254.

Deutscher, I. *What we say/what we do.* Glenview, Ill.: Scott, Foresman, 1973.

Ehrlich, H. J. Attitudes, behavior, and intervening variables. *American Sociologist,* 1969, *4,* 29–34.

Hill, R. Decision-making and the family life cycle. In G. F. Streib (Ed.), *Social Structure and the Family,* Englewood Cliffs, N.J.: Prentice-Hall, 1965.

Jones, E. E.; Kanouse, D. E.; Kelley, H. H.; Nisbett, R. E.; Valins, S.; & Weiner, B. *Attribution: Perceiving the causes of behavior.* Morristown, N.J.: General Learning Press, 1971.

Kelley, H. H. Attribution theory in social psychology. In D. Levine (Ed.), *Nebraska symposium on motivation,* 1967. University of Nebraska Press, 1967.

Kenkel, W. F. Observational studies of husband-wife interaction in family decision-making. In M. B. Sussman (Ed.), *Sourcebook in marriage and the family*, pp. 144-156. Boston: Houghton Mifflin, 1963.

Kuenzli, A. E. (Ed.). *The phenomenological problem*. New York: Harper & Bros., 1959.

Larson, L. E. System and subsystem perception of family roles. *Journal of Marriage and the Family*, 1974, *36*, 123-138.

Levinger, G. Supplementary methods in family research. *Family Process*, 1963, 2, 357-366.

Levinger, G. A three-level approach to attraction: Toward an understanding of pair relatedness. In T. L. Huston (Ed.), *Foundations of interpersonal attraction*. New York: Academic Press, 1974.

McCord, J., & McCord, W. Cultural stereotypes and the validity of interviews for research in child development. *Child Development*, 1961, *32*, 171-185.

McFall, R.M. Effects of self-monitoring on normal smoking behavior. *Journal of Consulting and Clinical Psychology*, 1970, *35*, 135-142.

Mogey, J. M. Research on the family: A search for world trends. *Journal of Marriage and the Family*, 1969, *31*, 225-232.

O'Dowd, M. M. Family supportiveness related to illicit drug immunity. Diss., University of Maryland, 1973.

Olson, D. H. The measurement of family power by self-report and behavioral methods. *Journal of Marriage and the Family*, 1969, *31*, 545-550.

Olson, D. H. Empirically unbinding the double bind: Review of research and conceptual reformulation. *Family Process*, 1972, *11*, 69-94.

Olson, D. H.; Berlin, J.; & Moyer, J. Communication training: Description and evaluation. Manuscript, University of Minnesota, 1975.

Olson, D. H., & Cromwell, R. C. Methodological issues in family power. In R. E. Cromwell & D. H. Olson (Eds.), *Power in families*. San Francisco: Sage & Halsted / Wiley, 1975.

Olson, D. H., & Rabunsky, C. Validity of four measures of family power. *Journal of Marriage and the Family*, 1972, *34*, 224-234.

Olson, D. H., & Straus, M. A. A diagnostic tool for marital and family therapy: The SIMFAM technique. *Family Coordinator*, 1972, *21*, 55-63.

Riley, M. W. Sources and types of sociological data. In R. E. L. Farris (Ed.), *Handbook of modern sociology*, pp. 978-1026. Chicago: Rand McNally, 1964.

Riskin, J. M., & Faunce, E. E. An evaluative review of family interaction research. *Family Process*, 1972, *11*, 365-455.

Ruano, B. J.; Bruce, J. D.; & McDermott, M. M. Pilgrim's progress II: Recent trends and prospects in family research. *Journal of Marriage and the Family*, 1969, *31*, 688-698.

Safilios-Rothschild, C. Family sociology or wives' family sociology? A cross-cultural examination of decision-making. *Journal of Marriage and the Family*, 1969, *31*, 290-301.

Safilios-Rothschild, C. The study of family power structure: A review 1960-1969. *Journal of Marriage and the Family*, 1970, *33*, 539-552.

Sanford, N. Will psychologists study human problems? *American Psychologist*, 1965, *20*, 192-202.

Snygg, C., & Combs, A. W. *Individual Behavior*. New York: Harper, 1949.

Straus, M. A. Measuring families. In H. T. Christensen (Ed.), *Handbook of marriage and the family*, pp. 335-400. Chicago: Rand McNally, 1964.

Turk, J. L., & Bell, H. W. Measuring power in families. *Journal of Marriage and the Family,* 1972, *34,* 215–222.

Wann, T. W. (Ed.). *Behaviorism and phenomenology.* Chicago: University of Chicago Press, 1964.

Webb, E. J.; Campbell, D. T.; Schwartz, R. D.; & Sechrest, L. *Unobtrusive measures.* Chicago: Rand McNally, 1966.

Weller, L., & Luchterhand, E. Comparing interviews and observations on family functioning. *Journal of Marriage and the Family,* 1969, *31,* 115–122.

Winter, W. D., & Ferreira, A. J. *Research in family interaction.* Palo Alto: Science and Behavior Books, 1969.

7
Re-Viewing the Close Relationship
GEORGE LEVINGER

What is a "close relationship"? Is it a merging of two bodies, as in the sex act? A meeting of minds, as when two individuals agree on something important to both of them? Doing a job together, as when two partners work shoulder to shoulder on a common task? Or is it an enduring interpersonal bond, beginning long ago and expected to last long into the future?

A close relationship may be all these things, but probably is none alone. A sex act can be as casual as a handshake. A meeting of minds may be transient and even self-alien—as during hypnosis or if a listener is spellbound by a powerful orator. A common task helps build interpersonal attraction, but its impact can differ greatly; for example, two neighbors may both be digging a tunnel to join their houses or they may be digging a drainage ditch to lead water away during a flood emergency. Nor does the mere length of a relationship determine its closeness; two spouses may drift apart but continue to live together in empty toleration.

Interpersonal closeness, then, is hardly unidimensional. As viewed in this volume, closeness implies "intimacy," understanding, commitment. Although several of the authors focus on marriage relationships, we have not limited our attention to the marital or, for that matter, the heterosexual relationship. We have not limited ourselves to contemporary meanings of closeness. We have, however, been concerned with trying to investigate its varied facets.

My present aim is to reconsider the multifaceted nature of close

I want to thank Jack Hewitt, Ted Huston, and Ann Levinger for their valuable comments on a previous draft of this chapter.

relationships, to review some biases of both their members and their observers in trying to understand them, and to explore a framework for organizing researchable questions. In his own concluding chapter, my colleague, Harold Raush, offers a somewhat different but complementary view of our topic.

Facets of the Close Relationship

Interpersonal closeness is generally some combination of social, physical, and psychological nearness. A definition which is implicit in the present papers contains at least the following components: (*a*) frequent interaction (*b*) between spatially near partners, (*c*) who share significant common goals, (*d*) exchange personal disclosures, and (*e*) care deeply about one another.

This implicit definition—one part social, one part physical, and three parts psychological—says a lot. Yet it says nothing about many other aspects of the interpersonal relationship—nothing about the physical attractiveness of the partners' looks, tone, touch, smell, or taste. It says nothing about the length or the future duration of a relationship, or of the symmetry of its partners' roles and resources, or of the support or the conflict derived from each member's external relationships.

Considering the many aspects of relationships, it seems that we must look at them from different angles; no single view is sufficient. Without pretending to exhaust all possibilities, let us here look at four different units which are each party to a relationship: (1) The individual partner, (2) the pair unit, (3) the social group, and (4) the larger society, which creates conditions that affect the closeness experienced in smaller units. For example, in attempting to understand a Person-Other relationship, we can focus on *P*'s or *O*'s individual actions, beliefs, or feelings; the joint functioning and properties of the two partners; the connections of their relationship in a web of kinship and acquaintanceship; and the larger societal context in which *P* and *O* have been socialized and where their relationship will continue to exist.

These four different facets of closeness are often considered separately. The individual level of analysis has traditionally been the province of the psychologist; at least since William James, psychologists have distinguished sharply between the self and the not-self.[1] The dyad

[1] Nevertheless, James noted that when we consider a person's self, "we are dealing with a fluctuating material; the same object being sometimes treated as a part of me, at other times as simply mine, and then again as if I had nothing to do with it at all" (1948, p. 177; originally published 1892).

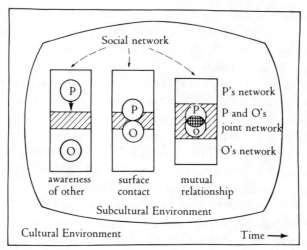

Figure 1. A Person-Other relationship in its sociocultural context (adapted from Huston & Levinger, in press)

is most often the focus of the social psychologist; for example, Cooley (1909) introduced the "we" to go along with James's "me." Social groups and networks are frequently the unit of the microsociologist, although social psychologists since Lewin have also been much interested in group interaction. Finally, societal and cultural levels of analysis are the concern of macrosociology, anthropology, and history; the societal level is the most resistant to precise analysis or to experiment.

Figure 1 permits us to look at these interrelations graphically. Individuals *P* and *O* exist as separate entities in the first and second frames (Awareness and Surface Contact), while in the third frame *P* and *O* have formed a pair relationship. Surrounding each individual, and later the pair, is each person's social network, which consists of relations to family, friends, colleagues at work, and other third parties; as a relationship develops between them, the two individuals' networks will come to overlap increasingly. Looking further, the societal level is the locus of one's subcultural and cultural environment. Finally, we must recognize that relations within and across these units of analysis are likely to change over time.

The Individual Western culture and Western social science often take an individualistic perspective on social behavior. We observe the single person as a unit, we question the individual actor, we hold individuals responsible for actions. And indeed individuals are the elemental builders and sustainers of relationships. Individual expectations and desires often determine the particular relationship sought; they shape satisfactions and frustrations, as well as desires to continue or to break particular relations. Individuals who are socialized in different cultures, subcultures, or families tend to relate rather differently.

Individuals also differ in their looks, their abilities, their resources, their goals, their personal dispositions. Some individuals are very attractive, others are unattractive. In every culture there are the stars and the isolates. Some people form social relations with ease, while others form them with difficulty; there are persons who form a few close relationships, and those who appear deprived of any.

The individual is the essential unit in Rosenblatt's and in Douvan's chapters. As Rosenblatt defines it, commitment is personal dedication; it is one person's intent to maintain a relationship. Rosenblatt's research questions about commitment in marriage derive from an individualistic cognitive consistency theory. While he considers pressures toward symmetry between two partners' commitment, he does not analyze symmetry elsewhere in their relationship—for instance, symmetry between the two partners' resources or their alternative opportunities. Nor does Rosenblatt examine the forces exerted by other members of a pair's social network or the demands fostered by a larger society. The individual perspective ignores these other aspects in order to enable investigators to design controlled objective research.

Yet Douvan, in her less research-oriented excursion, also emphasizes mainly individual variables. Although she suggests that America's fascination with individualism is an impediment to forming "true" relationships, she herself describes interpersonal relationships in terms of such individual variables as dependence, risk taking, and willingness to yield power to a partner. And she tends to consider individual personality differences in order to arrive at some of her generalizations.

Even in Levinger's chapter, where an attempt is made to construct a dyadic model to represent a "ship" which contains the relationship, individual variables such as involvement and commitment are offered as qualifiers of closeness. To study such feelings of involvement, the investigator must ask questions of individual respondents.

How do individuals define closeness? Probably they define it in terms of approaching another, finding a response from another, even losing one's self in the other. Individual definitions of closeness may be self-oriented or they may be other-oriented. Nonetheless, they are held in the eye of the perceiver, in the voice of the speaker, in the heart of the seeker. They are unilateral versions of one's feeling about another. They lead individuals to initiate encounters; they are implicit in idealizing another (Kerckhoff & Davis, 1962; Rubin, 1973) and in temporary feelings of arousal or passion (Berscheid & Walster, 1974). Unless properly reciprocated, however, such individual conceptions are likely to be unstable and reversible. Reciprocity and stability of closeness are, of course, not valued by everyone. Young people today are questioning the desirability of permanence in intimate relationships. Many prefer to merely harmonize or tune in with a partner for a limited engagement, while deliberately avoiding interpersonal commitments or entanglements.

Sex differences   Men and women, in our culture and in most others, have tended to differ strikingly in their expectations of closeness. At least until recently, men generally have been more concerned with material achievement and women with care and nurturance (Zelditch, 1955). In the present volume, Douvan suggests that the American male's historically based strivings for independence have interfered with his ability to absorb himself into a sharing relationship. Levinger notes that even today husband-wife differences in opportunities outside their marriage are sources of asymmetry and strain. Closeness, then, is likely to have different rewards and costs for members of either sex.[2]

Rubin (1973, 1975) has argued that it is generally less costly for men than for women to initiate and to enter romantic relationships; and following their establishment, it is usually more costly for women than for men to continue an unsatisfying association. Rubin's findings from a longitudinal study of premarital couples suggest that women tend to invest more of themselves in a relationship and therefore have more stake in its success.

This hypothesis of women's greater investment in relationships fits

[2]In her comments on Douvan's and Levinger's papers, Jessie Bernard also expressed concern with the differences between males and females in approaching interpersonal relations. She noted that men emphasize separation and repression, while women emphasize communion and openness; such sex differences are already visible in the classroom behavior of eight-year-olds. Yet Bernard also pointed to a paradox: Men's social relationships often are facilitated by their instrumental connections, their clubs, teams, committees, or hunting expeditions; while women's relationships are less often supported by such external structures or activities. In her book on the future of marriage, therefore, Bernard (1972) has written about the sharply different needs and resources that men and women bring to the marital relationship.

with Douvan's suggestion that women form richer and less restrained ties with other women than they form with men—or than men form with each other. It also fits with data from my own research program, where we find that female undergraduates rate their friendships significantly closer than do males and are more cognizant of both the rewards and the costs in their relationships.

The Dyad   The dyad, it has been said many times, is more than two times a single individual; it also contains the *relation between* self and other. Pairs are the smallest possible unit in which to observe interpersonal communication, conflict, agreement, or other forms of interaction. The three frames of figure 1 show a progression from an individualistic to a pair-centered emphasis. In the first frame, *P* sees *O* as an object that may or may not be rewarding; *P*'s own needs for individual gratification govern his or her perceptions. The second *P-O* frame depicts pair interaction, but the interaction is between two separate individuals; its discontinuation would leave each person intact, ready to resume an affiliation with someone else. The third frame, on the other hand, represents a true pair relationship; the intersection between the two circles depicts a substantial degree of *P-O* mutual interdependence.

The relation between *P* and *O* would seem to be the locus of social psychological analysis. In established relationships, however, it is rarely possible to differentiate clearly between initiator and respondent—to decide which partner is the cause of any given action (Watzlawick, Beavin, & Jackson, 1967). While social psychologists have studied interaction in the established pair to some extent, it has until now received a far lower share of attention than the superficial relation (Huston & Levinger, forthcoming). Our present volume is part of an effort to redress that imbalance.

In a commentary on papers in this volume, Alice Rossi noted that studies of intimate pairs have generally neglected the sensual side of the interaction. Expanding on a schema suggested by Mazur (1973), Rossi suggested that we distinguish among degrees of closeness according to the sense organs that are involved. Her continuum of intimacy begins with ear and eye contact between two persons; such contact can range from the casual to the very close. Sensual intimacy involves more than ear and eye; it also includes the senses of scent, touch, and taste, as in the activity of the nose, hands, and lips. Most intimate on Rossi's continuum is the contact of sexual organs; here all the previous senses participate in the mutual exploration, but also there is erotic contact of mouth, tongue, breast, and genitals. While the ear and the eye can operate at a distance, other modes of sensory interaction require physical nearness; furthermore, these latter forms of exchange are peculiarly suited to interaction in pairs rather than in larger groups. Rossi, therefore, has suggested that future research on pair relations give more recognition to the experience of sensory closeness.

Rossi's suggestion is difficult to follow directly, for one hesitates to expose intimate interaction to systematic observation. A recent study by Marylyn Lacey (1976), however, investigated such dyadic behaviors indirectly. Lacey was interested in people's "implicit theories" of interaction in typical pairs of twenty-two-year-olds. She showed her respondents lists of thirty different social behaviors and asked them to estimate the probability that they would occur in fourteen typical pair relations varying in degree of closeness and in sex composition. Half of her respondents were college students; the other half were senior citizens who averaged about fifty years older (and who rated the relationships for when they themselves were twenty-two years old). Lacey's study confirmed that intimate sensory interaction is expected to covary with degree of closeness; that, in the same-sex pairs, it is considered more likely to occur between female friends than between male friends; and that, in almost all of the relationships, it is believed to be more acceptable between twenty-two-year-olds today than in such pairs fifty years ago.

Before we turn to the larger social group in which pair relationships are embedded, I should like to note some distinctive features of the dyad in contrast with groups of larger size. Many years ago, Georg Simmel (1908) wrote that the dyad is the true locus of intimacy; its members are not distracted by the presence of others, and they know that both partners are necessary for the unit's continuation—which is not so in groups of three or more members. We may speculate that the members of the isolated pair are aware of its fragility and that pair members are more careful not to irritate one another than are members of larger groups. Two separate small group studies (Bales & Borgatta, 1955; O'Dell, 1968) have confirmed such a hypothesis in the laboratory, finding that the behavior of dyads differed significantly from that of groups of three to seven members. For example, O'Dell observed that pairs showed more tension and "interacted more slowly than larger groups" (1968, p. 77). And Bales and Borgatta (1955) found that members of dyads were less likely to show disagreement or antagonism than were those of other groups. It seems appropriate, then, to examine close relationships in the context of the larger social group.

The Social Group   Just as individuals can be considered to imply dyads—in the sense that any "self" always implies an "other"—so we may conceive of pairs as really triads.[3] For one thing, each pair is part of a larger group, such as a family or an acquaintance network. Also, whenever two people unite as a pair, they explicitly or implicitly react to third parties or outside social objects.

In the vocabulary of balance theory, persons P and O relate to each other via a common reference point X (Heider, 1946, 1958; Newcomb, 1953). That third element X may be another person, a thing, an activity, an idea, a myth. Two partners' correspondence about X tends to strengthen their relation, while their disagreement is a source of friction.

A group perspective looks beyond the dyad to the triad or larger network in which it is embedded (Ackerman, 1963; Bott, 1957; Kanter, Jaffe, & Weisberg, 1975; Slater, 1963). It suggests questions often neglected in the study of mere dyads: For example, how do members of a dyad tread the line between maintaining their own mutuality and weakening their relationship toward the rest of their group? To what extent is the pair relationship either supported or infringed upon by its strong connections to other members of the network—or by connections among those others themselves (Bott, 1957)? To what extent will "dyadic withdrawal" threaten the maintenance of the larger group?

There are no definitive answers to these questions. Considering "conjugal roles" in English married couples, Bott (1957) hypothesized that there is an inverse association between a couple's mutuality or closeness and the "connectedness" of their social network. This association is probably affected by still other variables—such as social class, occupation, geographic mobility, or sex-role ideology. Nonetheless, our memberships and our reference groups surely exercise an

---

[3]Lynn Hoffman commented at length on the importance of third parties in affecting pair relationships. She and Rosabeth Kanter both suggested that students of intimacy have paid insufficient attention to the influence of external relations or of the partners' wider networks.

important influence on our intimate relationships—and, in turn, our relationships shape our integration into such groups.

Turning to the *P-O* relationship depicted in figure 1, the two partners' separate networks in the first and second frames often become joint connections as a mutual relationship develops. It remains uncertain, though, how strengthening the dyad contributes to or detracts from the cohesiveness of the larger network. To assess that, we must turn to an examination of the wider culture.

The Society If one examines the interaction of pairs, families, and other groups, one can hardly avoid seeing the important influence played by forces emanating from the larger society. Sociologists and family historians have occasionally studied the effects of societal changes on intimate relations in the family (e.g., Goode, 1963; Shorter, 1975). Psychologists, on the other hand, have tended to consider close relationships apart from their wider context; we have usually limited our focus to microstructures. Gadlin's contribution to the present volume helps to expand our vision. In his delineation of changes in intimacy over different periods in American history, he shows vividly that meanings of closeness do not remain fixed. Gadlin's review reminds us that current forms of relationship reflect transitory historical effects.

Figure 1 has already indicated that intimate relationships and social networks are all part of a subcultural and cultural milieu. They are shaped by social institutions such as the economy, housing patterns, modes of communication and transportation. And therefore their form changes from one era to another.

Imagine another era or another culture in which husband and wife share the same work place, as on a small farm or in a business in the home. In such a society there would be high continuity between the work relationship and the couple's social-emotional ties. Such continuity provides stability and security, but it can also at times feel oppressive. Intimacy here is part of a larger whole, but it offers little escape from one part of one's life to another. Today, when many Americans appear alienated from their work, the pursuit of interpersonal intimacy seems to provide a refuge from the work place; nonetheless, Gadlin indicates that there is no ultimate escape.

The conditions under which people conduct their "private" relationships, then, are strongly affected by their economic and technological environment. The very concept of privacy means little if all one's interaction is under surveillance. That was true centuries ago in the crowded colonial household; it is also true today in various non-Western cultures, including modern China.

Interconnections   We have examined four different ways of looking at closeness and have considered some of their implications. One comes to realize that research on this topic is either explicitly or implictly affected by each of these varying views.

Before turning to look at some emerging research issues, however, I should like to consider Kelley's and Olson's methodological contributions to our volume. Their papers offer still another way of distinguishing among the alternative approaches to studying relationships. Each paper, in its own way, contrasts the views of inside members and outside observers.

The Relation between the Observed and the Observer

Transactions in close relationships are rather inaccessible to research. The members of a relationship are blind to some of its peculiarities; they have few bases for deciding when their relation is either typical or atypical. Nor are researchers entirely unbiased; they too are subject to the idiosyncrasies of their own backgrounds, are limited by the disclosures revealed by the members of the relationship, and are susceptible to attributional difficulties that arise from the very nature of the participant-observer relation.

Such limitations have important implications for designing research on close relationships, implications which are examined in Kelley's and Olson's methodological chapters. Before considering any research ideas, let us review the major points of those two chapters.

Attribution Theory   Kelley points to the "attributional processes" that occur in relationships; contrasting explanations of one's own and the other's behaviors are often associated with interpersonal conflict. Not only participants but also researchers make attributions when they observe persons or relationships and when they try to establish causal dynamics. Kelley suggests that the attributions of participants and of researchers follow the same laws, even though the researcher's method is an attempt to go beyond naive attribution.

Principles for predicting any specific attributional outcome derive from the particular combination among three elements: (*a*) actor or observer *consensus*, (*b*) target *distinctiveness*, and (*c*) *consistency* across situations. That is, an event that occurs only for one particular actor (low consensus) toward a wide range of targets (low distinctiveness) over many occasions (high consistency) tends to be seen as characteristic of the actor. An event in which most actors behave similarly (high consensus) but uniquely toward a particular target (high distinctiveness), and do so consistently across varying situations (high consistency), will be attributed to a characteristic of the target. Or an event that occurs for a single actor (low consensus) in regard to a particular target (high distinctiveness), and which has not occurred at other occasions (low consistency), is attributed to the peculiar circumstances of the situation.

While Kelley's examples are clear in theory, in real dyadic relationships it is often unclear who is the initiator (actor) and who is the target; in such cases, a straightforward attributional analysis may not be feasible.[4] Furthermore, while attribution theory is clearly testable when it is applied to specified ascriptions, such as those constructed in a research questionnaire—for example, "Hardly anyone else criticized Edward's conduct" or "Almost all other husbands also are unable to repair this toaster"—in real life such ascriptions are themselves attributions which themselves evolve out of attributional laws. In real life, one sometimes faces a sort of infinite regress—as when, for example, one asks: "How consensual is my judgment about consensus?"[5]

Researchers, Observers, and Actors Researchers too are observers. The second half of Kelley's chapter considers the researcher's own attributions. Kelley notes that the participants in a relationship see

[4]These points were made by Robert Leik, in his commentary on Kelley's paper. Furthermore, Leik wished to conceive observers' attributions in terms of continua, rather than via the dichotomies usually employed by attribution researchers. He outlined a way of translating Kelley's discrete "analysis of variance" model into a different causal model amenable to continuous variation and appropriate for multiple regression analysis.

[5]Attributions, as Kelley notes, reflect notions of causality. Conceptions of causality were also developed in Robert Weiss's commentary, which noted that the concept *cause* has varying meanings. There have been historical changes in the loci of cause—the gods, humors, inherited temperament, character, personality, social forces, and so forth. Our conception of causal attribution, then, is itself a likely object of historical change. Other discussants, especially Robert Ryder, were also concerned with the variations in the use of

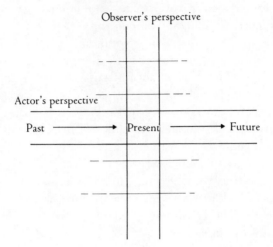

Figure 2. The differing perspectives of actors and observers

themselves in terms of events that occur in diverse situations over an extended period of time. Researchers, in contrast, usually see behavior in a restricted range of situations for a very limited time span, but typically across a wide range of individuals and relationships. Kelley's analysis indicates why observers tend to see a pair's behavior differently from the way the actors themselves see it. The basis for this difference is depicted in figure 2.

The horizontal axis in figure 2 refers to the temporal dimension which is assumed to affect actors' perceptions of their present interaction. Their viewpoint extends from their past into an anticipated future. The two partners are aware of both stability and change in their own relationship; they see how today differs from yesterday and also how it might differ from tomorrow. For example, if they consider today's quarrel a minor idiosyncracy in their pair's history or usual harmony, they are likely to attribute it to a peculiarity of their present situation. As Kelley notes, the partners' data about their own relationship are derived from the previous times and situations in which

the word *cause*. At times, cause is a statement of necessary and sufficient antecedents to an event; at times, it is a way of organizing phenomena into a pattern; at times, it is a statement about attribution to a responsible agent, as in blame. The term is used also for heuristic or mnemonic purposes. Furthermore, cause may be viewed in terms of single events or in terms of chains of long-range processes.

they have interacted with each other. These same partners, however, have limited knowledge about how their relationship compares with those of other pairs. They have observed interaction in pairs of their acquaintances and friends, but usually under different circumstances than their own. Thus it is difficult for two partners *systematically* to compare their own interaction with that in other pairs.

The viewpoint of the research observer is conceived to be orthogonal to that of the participants. The observer sees a single pair's interaction only in the context of the specific research situation and compares it to other relationships seen in the same circumstance and at the same time. The observer gathers data across relationships and across persons but has little access to situational variation; he rarely follows a pair over a long enough time span to make adequate longitudinal inferences. In Kelley's terms, an observer is led to favor assumptions of intersituational consistency of people and relationships; not knowing how different situations elicit behavior differences, his easiest assumption is that behavior remains consistent. And, assuming such consistency—as well as high interobserver consensus—observers tend to attribute differences across pairs to the enduring dispositions of the actors.

Since the typical observational method, then, seems biased toward personal attribution, Kelley suggests that alternative methods (and alternatives to a person-cause hypothesis) arportant for conducting research on close relationships. More attention to the actors' own introspections may help counteract the observer's biases.

Degrees of "Insiderness"   If attributions are strongly affected by being either "inside" or "outside" a relationship, Olson's chapter elaborates on such effects. He argues that the "subjective reality" of inside perspectives and the "objective reality" of outside perspectives are both essential for understanding close relationships.

Olson considers four contrasting research methods and emphasizes those two which have been used most often—self-report and behavioral observation. (He also notes that many studies purporting to investigate dyadic or familial relationships have been based entirely on self-reports from only one partner or family member, generally a wife or mother.) Olson further reviews the discrepancies between self-report and behavioral observation data in studies of decision-making power. Rather than rejecting self-report data, he points to the importance of both types of measures for tapping different aspects of reality.

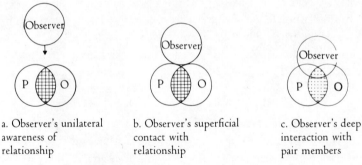

a. Observer's unilateral   b. Observer's superficial   c. Observer's deep
awareness of   contact with   interaction with
relationship   relationship   pair members

Figure 3. Degrees of an observer's "insiderness"

Let me build on some of Olson's ideas and propose a continuum of "insiderness" or objectivity-subjectivity.[6] This continuum is hard to demarcate because there are few markers for showing whether an observer is a distant viewer or an influential member of the observed relationship. Nevertheless, it is possible to sketch contrasting schemata of an observer's degree of insiderness.

The same Person-Other relationship is shown in each of the three frames of figure 3, but the three frames differ in the observer's relation to the P-O pair. In frame 3a, the observer stands entirely outside the relationship; his perception of P and O is as though he were watching unobtrusively through a window. In this situation of "unilateral awareness," the observer's interpretations of the partners' conduct are based on his preexisting knowledge of their culture, their situation, and his expectations of what interactants do. The "test" of his attributions derives from how well their observed conduct "fits" with his expectations.

In frame 3b, the observer and the pair interact, but their contact is superficial; an example would be a survey interview in which the interviewer asks rather impersonal questions of a pair of people he has just met. Here the observer's attributions are also based on his prior knowledge, but he makes an effort to verify them via the subjective response of the observed—by their answers to his questions. (A potential defect of survey interviewing is that the interviewer's questions may be so structured or sequenced as t exert a subtle influence on the answers of the respondent. The interviewer elicits the answers he seeks, but they may be erroneous.)

[6]This continuum was first suggested in Leik's comments on Olson's paper.

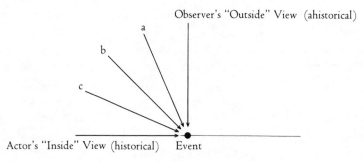

Figure 4. Varying views of the same event

In frame 3*c*, the observer-target relationship is intimate; for instance, a good friend who knows a couple closely gets information directly from one or both partners. Here the observer's attributions are put to a different sort of test. The participant observer assigns meaning to the acts of others and then acts toward them on that basis. Our test of meaning is pragmatic: If interaction proceeds as we have expected, then our assigned meaning of the other's act was correct. Unfortunately, we can be misled: The intended meaning of another's act is not self-evident; yet we can assign erroneous meaning and get responses that appear to confirm our expectations. (If I am suspicious of another person's "evil" motives, it is hard for me *not* to see confirmation of my own paranoia in any of his acts.) Perhaps varying degrees of distance and closeness are desirable in observer-actor relations; each degree of insiderness has both its limitations and its advantages.[7]

Insiderness and the Attributions of Observers   While Kelley's actor is at the extreme of insiderness, his observer displays extreme outsiderness. Within the language of figure 3, it seems possible to display different observer perspectives as they rotate from complete insiderness to complete outsiderness. Figure 4 pictures that. Its horizontal axis shows the actor's perspective, while its vertical axis depicts that of uninformed observers who see the actor behave at any single moment. Between those orthogonal extremes lie *degrees* of insiderness.

[7]In the hypothetical situation in fig. 3, the observer has equal contact with both members of the pair. This differs from the situation of many research studies where observers draw all their inferences from the behavior or the reports of merely one member. Even when observers try to represent all members of the unit they study, they receive unequal amounts of information from different members. (From a dyadic or a group perspective, of course, this inequality itself is useful information.)

Arrow *a* describes the perspective of an observer who has only a little more knowledge than that obtainable in a momentary exposure. People who are rather unfamiliar with the actor, but who see a sizable time slice of his behavior, have their perspective described by arrow *b*. Observers very close to the actor may share nearly the same perspective; thus their perspective nearly parallels the actor's own (arrow *c*).

The vertical axis in figure 4 describes a theoretical rather than a real instance. The real observer from our own culture shares so many of an actor's own assumptions and perspectives that it is nearly impossible for him not to be influenced by cross-situational viewpoints. The theoretical extreme best describes the hypothetical observer from a different culture (the hypothetical Martian?) who is entirely un-aware of the behavior stream in which the subjects' present interaction flows.[8]

In studying close relationships—and perhaps any topic of high salience to research subjects—investigators are often more "inside" than they expect to be. Furthermore, the very process of investigation has an impact on the relationships themselves. This not only raises issues of research ethics but also requires a conceptual treatment of the researcher-subject relationship as a component in our studies.[9] The stance of researcher vis-à-vis subject in terms of power, openness, and negotiation affects data gathering, analysis, and interpretation. One may question not only whether researchers are outside the phenomena they study but also whether they *should* be.

[8]Nancie Gonzalez commented on the ethnographer's problem as that of an outsider entering into the subjective viewpoint of the people s/he is studying. From this starting point, the ethnographer tries to "derive the rules and the categories by means of which the natives' reality is structured." Using the framework of ethnoscience, Gonzalez put the insider-outsider dimension into a hierarchical order. Insider perspectives are converted into the ethnographer's "emic" categories—the categories which name and describe from *within* the culture's own system. In contrast, the scientist's "etic" classifications represent an abstractive leap from an insider- to an outsider-perspective—an attempt to place particulars from a given culture into broader generalities *across* many cultures. Gonzalez noted that discussions of close relationships are confounded by a failure to distinguish whether our discourse is about emic or etic concepts.

[9]Zick Rubin commented on this problem from the standpoint of his own longitudinal couples research, in which couples were asked how their relationship had been affected by their research participation (Rubin, Peplau, & Hill, in preparation). Since couples' relationships often appeared affected by the insights they achieved while answering the researchers' questions, Rubin suggested that couples research may verge on couples counseling (see Rubin & Mitchell, 1976).

Beyond momentary assessment?   If we acknowledge, then, the observer's unavoidable contamination by "inside" nonobjectivity, can we endorse the pervasive tendency among researchers to capture only momentary cross-sections of interaction and structure in close relationships? Or shall we encourage a greater emphasis on longitudinal research, where observers will be able to follow changes over time? Furthermore, will researchers begin to attend to other temporal aspects of relational change—including seasonal, monthly, and even daily (or weekday-weekend?) fluctuations in relationships?

What Are Prospects for Research?

After reading this far, is anyone still tempted to plunge into research on close relationships? Having acknowledged the many different units of analysis, as well as the discrepancies between the data that are available to participants and researchers, how and whither can we suggest new directions?

The definition of research problems is not easy in this area. In other areas of social science there seem to be bodies of established fact and principle, where one's research problem is mainly to fill gaps or to extend the perimeter of knowledge. That is not so here.

For one thing, the study of close relationships falls at the crossing of many paths to understanding. Directions and interconnections among these paths are disputable, and there is no map for exploring a demarcated region. Furthermore, our knowledge regarding narrower, more definable subregions such as mate selection or marriage is largely normative and culture-bound; it is difficult to estimate how findings in those areas are affected by changes in the economy, in the welfare system, in technology and communication, or in societal living arrangements. Here, I can try merely to make some suggestions to help us acknowledge these interconnections.

A Matrix for Generating Research Questions   The four contrasting levels of analysis reviewed earlier—the units of individual, pair, group, and society—are complementary to each other. Most research on close relationships, however, focuses on only one level to the neglect of others. Recalling our earlier discussion of attribution theory, it would appear that the researcher who favors an objective or "outside" perspective is tempted to make attributions to personal dispositions,

Table 1   A Matrix for Generating Questions about Close Relationships

	1. Individual	2. Dyad	3. Group	4. Society
1. Individual	1,1	1,2	1,3	1,4
2. Dyad	2,1	2,2	2,3	2,4
3. Group	3,1	3,2	3,3	3,4
4. Society	4,1	4,2	4,3	4,4

while one who prefers a subjective or "inside" stance would perceive causes as emanating primarily from the situation or the environment.

It is noteworthy, then, that Rosenblatt—whose chapter here espouses an objective hypothesis-testing pursuit of social science—focuses his conceptual lens at the individual-cognitive level. Rosenblatt states his research questions in terms of individual choices, acts, and commitments. Contrast his approach with that of Gadlin, whose paper attributes the forms and actions of intimacy to influences from the participants' environmental constraints.[10] We may wonder whether Rosenblatt's and Gadlin's opposing viewpoints are derivable from Kelley's attribution theory?

In the remainder of this section, I try to bridge the four different perspectives on closeness. I attempt to look at the connections among individual, dyadic, group, and societal variables as the source of questions for research. To do so, let us imagine the four-by-four matrix in table 1. On the left side, heading the rows of the matrix, each unit appears successively as the source of "causes;" each column head, in turn, refers to the source of "effects."[11] In the first row, then, we would ask how variables at the individual level interact with variables at each of the four levels of analysis. To illustrate this, let us see how one variable—an individual's personal autonomy—might affect well-being at the level of each unit. Thus we consider questions in row 1.

1. Individual autonomy   Autonomy is a personal quality highly valued in Western society, but it is not desirable under all conditions. A research question that arises in cell$_{1,1}$, then, is the following one: Under

[10]In his informal remarks during our conference, Gadlin emphasized how much he, as actor, feels caught inside the very phenomena about which we are here trying to pursue generalizations.

[11]Strictly speaking, we should not speak of cause or effect, and I do so here only for reasons of exposition. Rather we must acknowledge the circularity of effects that permeate this matrix.

what conditions does high autonomy enhance personal well-being, and under what conditions will it diminish such well-being? High degrees of autonomy promote task achievement and enhance personal power, but intermediate autonomy is more conducive for initiating and maintaining satisfactory social relationships (see Douvan's chapter). How do individuals walk the path between counterdependency and overdependency? How do their personalities determine how they resolve the dilemma between interpersonal enmeshment and personal isolation?

In cell$_{1,2}$, we would ask how personal autonomy affects interpersonal harmony in the dyad. If two partners' expressions of autonomy fit well with each other, then each one's independence would enrich the relationship. In what ways, though, do private moves toward autonomy generate tendencies toward pair deterioration and breakup? When do personal alternatives outside a relationship (Levinger, 1976) enrich it, and when do they impoverish it?

Cell$_{1,3}$, would encourage questions about the effects of individual members' actions on events and emotions in the group. Individual withdrawal in a twosome leads to its destruction, but the survival of groups larger than two is not dependent on any single member. Again, autonomy of particular members may both enrich and threaten the larger unit—although its effects on a larger group are weaker than on a dyad.

Cell$_{1,4}$ alludes to the effects of individual actions on one's larger social environment. The wider the society, the less immediate are the effects of any single person's actions or intentions—unless the actor occupies an especially potent position. Nonetheless, the aggregation of many similar individual actions does affect total society.

2. *Pair "unity"*   Let us now consider row 2 of our matrix. Our causal variable will now be the "unity" of a pair, as analogous to the autonomy of the individual. Unity here means unit-y—the extent to which a pair operates as a unit rather than as two separate persons.

Cell$_{2,1}$ pertains to its effect on individuals, either the pair members themselves or its nonmembers. Do members of a pair feel increasingly supported or increasingly constrained as unity grows? What are the limiting conditions for such effects? In what ways does partnership serve as an important source of self-definition?

A pair's unity is a source of strength and of weakness. Carried to its extreme—for example, in "closed marriage" as caricatured by advocates of "open marriage"—exaggerated pair sufficiency becomes insufficiency.

In a world of shifting experience, ingrown partnerships are vulnerable to the awakening of new individual needs; what was earlier a reason for gratification can later become a source of stultification. In such a world, pair "renewal" becomes a personal problem.

Cell$_{2,2}$ represents the locus of many vital research issues. There is burgeoning literature on pair communication and couple conflict which looks at pair variables as they affect other pair variables. The thinking here is interactional or systemic; cause and effect are fully intertwined. Thibaut and Kelley's (1959) introduction of the dyadic outcome matrix has inspired much thinking about such interactional issues (e.g., Carson, 1969; Levinger & Huesmann, in press); other work has been oriented toward communication theory (e.g., Raush, Barry, Hertel, & Swain, 1974; Watzlawick, Beavin, & Jackson, 1967). Research on the modification of pair conflict is also now beginning to concentrate at this dyadic level (Gottman, Notarius, Markman, Bank, Yoppi, & Rubin, 1976; Weiss, Hops, & Patterson, 1973).

Let us turn to the remaining cells in the second row. In cell$_{2,3}$, one would ask about the effects of pair unity on group cohesion; in cell$_{2,4}$ we would be concerned with its impact on the wider society. If the network is very small, such as the nuclear family, the pair's harmonious continuity is likely to be important—as a source either of stability or of dyadic withdrawal. For the wider network, dyadic unity and disunity have only aggregate effects. They are the source of demographic statistics—they contribute to the marriage rate and the divorce rate, to welfare and court statistics.

3. *Group connectedness*   By now, the reader may prefer to journey alone through the remainder of table 1. Its matrix was conceived more to stimulate than to invent a complete research program. Nonetheless, I will pose a few questions pertinent to rows 3 and 4.

In row 3, we may ask how connectedness of any social network will affect individual, pair, group (the network itself), and the larger society? At each level it is likely to be a source of both positive and negative effects. For example, the individual—whether child or adult— will find a closely knit network a source of security but also a source of domination and a drain on resources.

In a lengthy review of the marriage literature in the second edition of her book, Bott (1971) has assessed findings about the association between network density and pair functioning. Effects of network connectedness are complex and remain a challenge for further investigation.

4. Congruity among societal institutions Degree of congruity among institutions illustrates the sort of variable that is pertinent to row 4 of the matrix. A completely congruent society would be a totalitarian utopia or dystopia. In such fiction, the insider is totally "in," the outsider is totally an outcast. We are familiar with such individual bliss and humiliation in the fictional societies of *Brave New World* and *1984*.

The societies or subsocieties of our real acquaintance, though, all contain incongruities among institutions and ideals. Deviation from one societal ideal generally implies and is supported by conformity to a different ideal. A societal perspective focuses on such incongruities as a source for analysis and critique.

Developmental Changes So far my questions have ignored changes over time. At each of the four levels it is possible, of course, to ask about dynamic processes of relational formation, maintenance, and dissolution. Longitudinal research has not been emphasized in this volume, but it is an important aspect of our topic. Although longitudinal studies are costly and difficult, they do supplement cross-sectional research. The systematic combination of cross-sectional and longitudinal assessment recently introduced by developmental researchers (e.g., Baltes, 1968) offers another possible approach.

At the individual level, one might ask how age affects changing desires for intimacy and isolation; Erikson's (1950) seminal suggestions have received little empirical study. At the pair level, one might do more to chart the multiple paths toward closeness and distancing; despite some exciting exceptions (Rubin, Peplau, & Hill, in preparation; Hetherington, Cox, & Cox, 1976), there are few current instances of excellent longitudinal research on the development or deterioration of intimacy. At the group and societal levels, longitudinal research may require new sorts of materials. Retrospective historical analysis seems to be one worthy method for further exploration.

Whatever the approach, I think it is important to improve our data-based understanding of intimate relationships. For, while many seek love and closeness, they often do not know how to find it—or how to hold it once it seems in their grasp.

A Personal Conclusion

When I first sat down with Harold Raush to plan the gathering which became the basis for the current volume, I was motivated by several concerns. To begin with, I felt that the topic of close relationships strikes centrally at every one of us; we are all researchers into intimate relationships insofar as we are members of the human race. Furthermore, the increasing pace of social change has altered traditional expectations to create a revolution in social norms and personal desires; we are all likely to be confused about the right and the wrong, the practical and the impractical, the eventual good and bad. Young and old alike seem ready to explore almost anything in the way of relationships, and to discontinue those that appear unsatisfactory.

When we were planning our two-day meeting, it seemed to me that social scientists would be able to speak clearly to these issues, to present theories and data that could help people to resolve some of their uncertainties. Looking today, I am impressed by the wisdom on many of the pages in this volume, but I also now view our topic with a greater humility. I now better understand the legitimacy of each of the differing perspectives. I see better how it is that social scientists and others often talk past one another. Not only is communication hampered by conflicting norms; it is also obscured by the orthogonal biases of actors and observers, and by the likelihood that differing disputants perceive their subject at differing levels of analysis. If one discussant operates at row 1, another at row 2 or 3, and a third looks in row 4 for the sources of effects, no wonder they disagree on priorities.

I am also nagged by a sense of personal discomfort. I am still motivated by my own need to bring integration between the conflicting desires people have toward interpersonal closeness. I remain troubled about my own need for autonomy and my need for strengthening social ties. The pursuit of personal power still struggles with the longing for interpersonal love.[12]

My feelings are captured in the following nostalgic account of a funeral. The writer, two generations younger than the deceased, Mary Jones, reminisces about the Joneses' close companionship during the course of their long marriage:

Their enjoyment of each other was arresting—sharp as pepper, golden. I have seen other happy old couples, but this picture of the

[12] This conflict is handled at much greater length in Harold Raush's concluding chapter.

Joneses, renewed many times, came to represent to me an essence of human exchange—something indescribably moving and precious, which comes to fruition only toward the end of a lifelong marriage. Whatever that essence is, I find it dazzling. It has always struck me as one of the great possibilities life has to offer. . . .

During Mary Jones's funeral, I basked in the thought of her marriage, hoarding the warmth against the astral chill of an unknown future. The future chilled me not because I think it promises to eradicate long, happy marriages from the face of the earth; only the most tyrannical social system could accomplish that. What chilled me was a more general sense of the transformation of our society from one that strengthens the bonds between people to one that is, at best, indifferent to them; a sense of an inevitable fraying of the net of connections between people at many critical intersections, of which the marital knot is only one. Each fraying accelerates others. A break in one connection, such as attachment to a stable community, puts pressure on other connections; marriage, the relationship between parents and children, religious affiliation, a feeling of connection with the past—even citizenship, that sense of membership in a larger community which grows best when it is grounded in memberships in a small one. If one examines these points of disintegration separately, one finds they have a common cause—the overriding value placed on individual emancipation and fulfillment, in the light of which, more and more, the old bonds are seen not as enriching but as confining. We are coming to look upon life as a lone adventure, a great personal odyssey, and there is much in this view which is exhilarating and strengthening, but we seem to be carrying it to such an extreme that if each of us is an Odysseus, he is an Odysseus with no Telemachus to pursue him, with no Ithaca to long for, with no Penelope to return to—an Odysseus on a journey that has been rendered pointless by becoming limitless. [The Talk of the Town, *The New Yorker*, August 30, 1976. pp. 21-22]*

Does commitment to self have primacy now over commitment to family and social bond? Is today's major goal self-development and self-actualization? So it may appear.

*From Notes and Comment in *The New Yorker*. Reprinted by Permission; © 1976 The New Yorker Magazine, Inc.

While life has always been lived in a tension between individual desire and group demand, it seems that in earlier times the group generally emerged the victor. Today the pendulum has swung the other way, fraying the connections that hold together the net of social relationships. But if the knots of our social fabric tear asunder, the individual will once again become the loser. If personal fulfillment is pursued to its extreme, it leads to eventual estrangement and emptiness.

I suggest that we seek solutions to our modern problem in the redefinition of the "self"—that "fluctuating material" discussed long ago by William James. One road toward attaining self-fulfillment may be the expansion of our personal boundaries. It would recognize not only the individual, but also the dyadic, the group, and the societal components of self. Such visions attract me as I contemplate the continuing exploration of close relationships.

References

Ackerman, C. Affiliations: Structural determinants of differential divorce rates. *American Journal of Sociology*, 1963, 69, 12–20.

Bales, R. F., & Borgatta, E. F. Size of group as a factor in the interaction profile. In A. P. Hare; E. P. Borgatta; & R. F. Bales (Eds.), *Small groups: Studies in social interaction.* New York: Knopf, 1955.

Baltes, P. B. Longitudinal and cross-sectional sequences in the study of age and generation effects. *Human Development*, 1968, 11, 145–171.

Bernard, J. *The future of marriage.* New York: World, 1972.

Berscheid, E., & Walster, E. A little bit about love. In T. L. Huston (Ed.), *Foundations of interpersonal attraction.* New York: Academic Press, 1974.

Bott, E. *Family and social network.* London: Tavistock, 1957 (2nd ed., 1971.)

Carson, R. C. *Interaction concepts in personality.* Chicago: Aldine, 1969.

Cooley, C. H. *Social organization.* New York: Scribner, 1909.

Erikson, E. H. *Childhood and society.* New York: Norton, 1950.

Goode, W. J. *World revolution and family patterns.* New York: Free Press, 1963.

Gottman, J.; Notarius, C.; Markman, H.; Bank, S.; Yoppi, B.; & Rubin, M. E. Behavior exchange theory and marital decision making. *Journal of Personality and Social Psychology*, 1976, 34, 14–23.

Heider, F. Attitudes and cognitive organization. *Journal of Psychology*, 1946, 21, 107–112.

Heider, F. *The psychology of interpersonal relations.* New York: Wiley, 1958.

Hetherington, E. M.; Cox, M.; & Cox, R. The aftermath of divorce. Paper, University of Virginia, 1976.

Huston, T. L., & Levinger, G. Interpersonal attraction and relationships. In M. R. Rosenzweig & L. W. Porter (Eds.), *Annual Review of Psychology*, vol. 29. Palo Alto, Calif.: Annual Reviews, in press.

James, W. *Psychology* (abridged ed.). New York: World, 1948 (originally published in 1892).

Kanter, R. M., Jaffe, D. T., & Weisberg, D. K. Coupling, parenting, and the presence of others: Intimate relationships in communal households. *The Family Coordinator*, 1975, *24*, 433-452.

Kerckhoff, A. C., & Davis, K. E. Value consensus and need complementarity in mate selection. *American Sociological Review*, 1962, *27*, 295-303.

Lacey, M. Implicit theories of relationship. Master's thesis, University of Massachusetts, Amherst, 1976.

Levinger, G. A social psychological perspective on marital dissolution. *Journal of Social Issues*, 1976, *32* (1), 21-47.

Levinger, G., & Huesmann, L. R. An "incremental exchange" perspective on the pair relationship: Interpersonal reward and level of involvement. In K. J. Gergen; M. S. Greenberg; & R. H. Willis (Eds.), *Social exchange: Advances in theory and research*. New York: Wiley, in press.

Mazur, R. M. *The new intimacy: Open-ended marriage and alternative life styles*. Boston: Beacon Press, 1973.

Newcomb, T. M. An approach to the study of communicative acts. *Psychological Review*, 1953, *60*, 393-404.

O'Dell, J. N. Group size and emotional interaction. *Journal of Personality and Social Psychology*, 1968, *8*, 75-78.

Raush, H. L.; Barry, W. A.; Hertel, R. K.; & Swain, M. A. *Communication, conflict, and marriage*. San Francisco: Jossey-Bass, 1974.

Rubin, Z. *Liking and loving*. New York: Holt, Rinehart, & Winston, 1973.

Rubin, Z. Loving and leaving. Paper, Harvard University, 1975.

Rubin, Z., & Mitchell, C. Couples research as couples counseling: Some unintended effects of studying close relationships. *American Psychologist*, 1976, *31*, 17-25.

Rubin, Z.; Peplau, L. A.; & Hill, C. T. *Becoming intimate: The development of male-female relationships*. In preparation.

Shorter, E. *The making of the modern family*. New York: Basic Books, 1975.

Simmel, G. In K. H. Wolff (Ed.), *The sociology of Georg Simmel*. New York: Free Press, 1950 (German ed. published in 1908).

Slater, P. E. On social regression. *American Sociological Review*, 1963, *28*, 339-358.

Thibaut, J. W., & Kelley, H. H. *The social psychology of groups*. New York: Wiley, 1959.

Watzlawick, P.; Beavin, J. H.; & Jackson, D. D. *Pragmatics of human communication*. New York: Norton, 1967.

Weiss, R. L.; Hops, H.; & Patterson, G. R. A framework for conceptualizing marital conflict. In L. A. Hamerlynck; L. H. Handy, & E. J. Marsh (Eds.), *Behavior change*. Champaign, Ill.: Research Press, 1973.

Zelditch, M., Jr. Role differentiation in the nuclear family. In T. Parsons & R. F. Bales (Eds.), *Family, socialization, and interaction process*. Glencoe, Ill.: Free Press, 1955.

8

Orientations to the Close Relationship

HAROLD L. RAUSH

Love, like matter, is much odder than we thought. — W. H. Auden

Editors of a volume on a specific topic, like this book on close relationships, may legitimately be asked for their conclusions from the collection of independent chapters. Yet, as must be apparent to the reader, no simple formulas emerge. The responsibility lies partly with the editors, who invited diversity in the orientation of the contributors. But also, as this diversity suggests, the fault is in the state of the subject matter. If we had thought to compare, contrast, and draw conclusions from different recipes for the same dish—called close relationship—we were sorely deluded. Our contributors have concocted very different dishes, in some cases whole menus, of ingredients that are sometimes but not always similar. A wide and varied repast, but not easily digestible.

Yet, to leave this analogy, although each chapter stands independently, some common themes do emerge. Rather than conclusions, these themes are recurring matters of concern. As identified by Levinger and myself in preliminary discussions, six major issues pervade these chapters. They influence the conceptualizations and point directions for further theory and research.[1] These issues can be put in the form of questions:

1. How do cultural and historical factors affect the nature of close relationships, and the way we conceive of them? A related issue has to do with how we examine cultural and historical continuities or changes in relationships.

[1]Summary analyses at the conference where the papers were presented by Reuben Hill and by Zick Rubin, contributed considerably to this classification.

2. What are the effects of internal and external constraints on close relationships? Do we conceive of and live our intimacies as freely chosen, personal actions? Or are these seemingly most private aspects of our lives determined primarily by social and economic structures and norms about which we have little choice? What are the connections between internal and external constraints? Do they stand in opposition to one another, or may they enhance one another? And what are the balances between them which may favor or oppose the formation and maintenance of close relationships?

3. How do our own values—either as participants or as researchers within a particular cultural milieu—affect our conceptions of close relationships? Are our research directions biased, for example, by implicit assumptions that stable, long-term, intensely intimate relationships are per se "good"? Are our investigations subtle defenses of the status quo? Do we orient toward social and personal change? Does our orientation to relationships emphasize individual autonomy or does it emphasize social integration? And how do our values toward one or the other of these goals affect research?

4. What shall be our unit for conceptual and research analysis? Do we focus on the individual participants in relationships, on the intimate pair, on the nuclear or extended family unit, on the face-to-face primary group, or on the total social community?

5. How does the investigator's perspective influence research approaches and findings? Does he/she view the close relationship from a position as coparticipant, and what differences result from these different perspectives? Who defines a close relationship? Is closeness that which is judged as such by the observer or by the participants themselves?

6. What dimensions or categories can best contribute to a framework for studying close relationships? Even aside from questions about specific variables, what is the range of relationships to be included— termporary or lasting sexual encounters, same-sex friendships, kinship arrangements?

These issues are not independent of one another. They overlap greatly. Moreover, they are not only substantive matters but also have methodological implications. As Kelley suggests in chapter 5, method has an intimate link with substance. One's orientation to these themes determines one's methodological approach to the study of close relationships.

In this "concluding" chapter I shall not comment equally on all these themes. My primary focus will be on the issues of internal and external constraints on relationships. Through the medium of that focus I shall touch, to a greater or lesser degree, on the other themes and on some methodological implications. A secondary focus will be toward considering some aspects that are relatively neglected in the preceding discussions but that are, I believe, essential to an understanding of close relationships. My hope is to develop, if only sketchily here, a framework for integrating some of the diversity in the preceding chapters and for leading to new directions for analysis. Before turning to this framework, I want to summarize the arguments, as they appear in this volume, so as to see where we now stand.

Part 1: Relationship and Constraint

A major theme noted above concerns the influence of cultural and historical factors on both nature and conceptualization of close relationships. Social changes in the conception and indeed the experience of intimacy are addressed most specifically in Gadlin's chapter, but Douvan and Levinger and to a lesser degree our other authors acknowledge the contexts that give rise to particular orientations to interpersonal relations. That recognition is reflected not only in an awareness of changing social values but also in at least some degree of attention to the effects of particular social and historical contexts on what researchers study and how they study it.

This theme of the connection between the social and the personal is elaborated into issues concerning the balance between internal and external constraints on the formation and maintenance of close relationships. The question of how social forces affect relationships pervades the chapters. For example, Levinger's primary concepts of involvement, commitment, and symmetry appear to be voluntaristic in orientation; they refer to choices of the individual participants in a relationship. Yet he notes that social norms are integral to closeness and that each of the three variables, as well as the dyadic pair itself, exists in a social context. Similarly, Rosenblatt, though examining commitment from the perspective of the individual, notes the effects of external forces as, for example, the presence of children.[2] Kelley's attributional

[2]In discussions, Jessie Bernard and Alice Rossi emphasized the power that external constraints exercise over relationships. Bernard noted particularly how social inequities in

analysis, while focused on the perceptions of individuals, depends heavily on external events; such events affect the observer's or the participants' impressions of *consensus, distinctiveness,* and *consistency.* Moreover, Kelley notes that observers are apt to attribute behavior to internal causes when information is lacking as to external constraint (his *discounting* principle) or when the behavior occurs despite external inhibitory influences (his *augmentation* principle).[3] Olson does not deal directly with the effects of internal versus external constraints, but his analysis is of a closely related issue: the differences in research data obtained from external versus internal perspectives on a relationship.

The two most radical positions on the connection between internal or external constraints and close relationships are represented by Gadlin and Douvan. Gadlin takes a strong historical determinist position: It is the public order, particularly the economic structure, that determines the circumstances, definitions, and vicissitudes of private intimacy. To exaggerate his view but slightly, personal leverage in the close relationship is primarily illusion. Douvan takes, in a sense, an opposite position. Although she notes clearly the historical and normative forces that shape relationships—particularly those between men and women in America—she resolves the issue of external versus internal constraints by defining the close relationship as nonnormative. For Douvan, the intimate relationship—admittedly idealized—is free from external and role-imposed constraints. Her emphasis is on the pleasure of the relationship itself, its spontaneity and freedom. Within her conceptualization—in which the single norm seems to be loyalty—the ideal model of intimacy is represented by friendship between two members of the

---

male-female norms affect men and women differentially in their attitudes and satisfactions in marriage. Rossi pointed to the general neglect of economic factors in analyses of relationships, and she illustrated how a consideration of economic and role constraints might be used to account for some seemingly paradoxical findings concerning the stresses of marriage. Rosabeth Kanter and Robert Ryder noted negative effects of external constraints on relationships and the contribution of such effects to what Kanter called the "tyranny of close relationships."

[3] Robert Weiss, in particular, noted in discussion the confusions that people undergo in making causal attributions as to external or internal forces. He finds, for example, that when relationships have been broken by death or divorce, persons are likely to attribute the difficulties of loneliness and of forming new relationships to their internal inadequacies, whereas in reality such difficulties are often more related to inadequacies and lacks in social institutions.

same sex.[4] Heterosexual relations, she implies, fall short of intimacy in that they are heavily constrained by what Gadlin calls the "public order."[5]

Douvan's emphasis on the nonnormativeness of intimate friendships accents the negative aspects of external constraints on closeness. Popular images of intimacy similarly emphasize its internal voluntary character. Although many studies show that socioeconomic and cultural variables play a large part in determining the initiation of relationships, the maintenance of psychological closeness is usually assumed to be more a matter of personal choice.[6] And although something is known about external forces that erode intimacy (e.g., economic deprivation, geographic or occupational mobility, etc.), there has been little study of the external conditions or role structures that enhance intimacy.

Internal and external influences on relationships have usually been put in an either-or fashion, as one focus versus the other. Their interconnections remain largely unexamined, although attribution theory (Kelley, this volume) may offer one approach to studying these linkages. As Levinger notes, there is all too little research on the association between external constraints and perceptions of autonomy and freedom.[7]

The relations of external/internal, inside/outside, personal experience/public order and the effects of these relations on perceptions of

[4]In discussions, a number of participants suggested that this model of intimacy between two friends of the same sex was more apt to be represented in women's than in men's relationships. Jourard's (1971) findings on differential self-disclosure by men and women provide some support for this view. Sex differences in patterns and experiences of friendship are, however, still a rather unexplored research area.

[5]Douvan's approach—which attempts to resolve the dialectic between external, societal constraint and internal, spontaneous choice through defining spontaneity as the prime component of intimacy—is reminiscent of similar resolutions in documents of medieval "Courts of Love" (see Lederer & Jackson, 1968, pp. 27–30). There too the argument ran that, since marriage involved contractual obligation, love could not exist within marriage. The solution of medieval nobility was to define love as heterosexual devotion outside the bond of marriage.

[6]As Rossi noted in discussion, recent economic analyses show the powerful force of external constraints on marital stability. Social exchange theory (Thibaut & Kelley, 1959) also suggests the influence of the availability of alternative resources on the maintenance of primary relationships.

[7]Haley (1963, p. 120) gives an illustration of this association. He suggests that in a relationship which is strongly bounded by external norms (as, for example, in a marriage where divorce is not morally or legally possible) participants may continually question

freedom or constraint preoccupy our authors. That relationships have both outside and inside worlds, and that these worlds may differ, indeed accords with our phenomenological experience—and with the research findings addressed by Olson. But the diversity of approaches to, and conclusions drawn about, these issues suggest that much remains unclear. For example, whether the discussion is on external versus internal forces or on their interconnections, at least two assumptions are often implied and unquestioned. One assumption is that external and internal factors of relationship are objectively distinguishable; the second assumption is that they may be conceptualized and studied as independent of each other. Moreover, both assumptions seem to coexist implicitly with simultaneous awareness, and often explicit discussions, of the internalization of social norms. Such confusions suggest a need for further analysis and clarification.[8]

Part 2: Orientations

Toward such clarification I want to suggest and explore three orientations to experience—the personal, the interpersonal, and the societal.[9] These orientations are frames through which the outside observer studies relationships; they are also the contexts through which participants view their own experiences. Whether we are examining the relationships of others or reflecting on our own, we are, I suggest, engaged in all three orientations simultaneously, in a dialectical process among them. Along with the dialectic among personal, interpersonal, and societal orientations is a second dialectic process that concerns shifting balances between internalization and externalization.

---

whether their commitment is voluntary or involuntary; in contrast, in the relationship which lacks external constraints, even the most minor of conflicts is apt to be seen as threatening to personal autonomy and as cause for disengagement.

[8]Further elaborations may be added to the inside-outside problem. Robert Leik, for example, in discussion emphasized the notion of continua and ranges of inside versus outside views and of subjectivity versus objectivity. Bernard pointed to further complexity in noting that external constraints transform interpersonal relationships and that the internal meanings of specific acts are altered by such transformations.

[9]Levinger, in chapter 7 herein, refers to four perspectives—differentiating between the perspective of the face-to-face group and the perspective of the social community. The distinction is an important one. It is only for the sake of limiting further complexity that I omit it here. Consideration of the influence of the face-to-face small group would somewhat modify the discussion that follows but would not alter major points.

From this point of view, the close relationship is best understood not as something that "is." Rather, it is a temporal and developmental process that derives from homeostatic balances in dialectics among alternative orientations and between internalization and externalization. This process represents not only our experiences of continuities and changes in close relationships but also historical and cultural continuities and changes in conceptions of close relationships.

The Personal Orientation   Before turning to the dialectical processes, we need to consider the three orientations. A ready illustration is to be found in the concept of commitment. The personal orientation is most clearly exhibited in Rosenblatt's chapter. Rosenblatt defines commitment as *an avowed or inferred intent of a person to maintain a relationship* (his italics). Now clearly Rosenblatt is aware of the multiple social forces that influence such an intent; indeed, he discusses these forces and suggests areas for research in the relations between commitment and marriage ceremonies, the presence of children, social norms, and situational changes. But his focus is on the individual: it is the individual's intent that is impacted by what are seen as external influences. Levinger, for whom the concept of commitment is also central to the close relationship, takes a position similar to Rosenblatt's in his emphasis on its personal, voluntaristic aspects;[10] he, too, refers to social norms as either enhancing or impeding individual commitment. Although Douvan's discussion of commitment is less formalized, and although her emphasis is more on spontaneity and risk taking in relationships, she shares with Rosenblatt and Levinger a perspective from the individual person.

The Societal Orientation   Before turning to the interpersonal, it may be useful to consider the contrast to the personal that is offered by a societal orientation to commitment. Commitment is most often thought of as a personal variable and is most often seen from a personal perspective; that is, it is the individual who commits himself/herself. But we may also look at commitment from a societal context. Barker's

[10]Levinger's position is somewhat ambiguous in that prior to his discussion of the concept he speaks of commitment as pertaining to the strength of the boundaries of a relationship. This notion, as well as the implications of the Lewinian representation in his fig. 2, moves commitment away from a personal perspective and toward a systems conception.

(1968) research demonstrates the powerful forces that social institutions and social structurings of space and time exert on people's involvement and commitment (see also Sarason, 1974). Schools, games, performances, all require commitment.

A societal orientation can be seen developmentally in the demands and boundaries set for the growing child. Family relationships and family norms—the ways a family both defines itself and is defined by its social community—call for more than passive compliance; they call for active commitment on the part of the child. So, too, integration into a peer culture presents a social demand for commitment. In adolescence, the social demands increase and diversify; and, indeed, a major problem for the adolescent is to resolve dilemmas of choices and restrictions among social—or antisocial—opportunities that beckon for commitment.

Intimacy also can be seen as a social demand, as a social statement of the opportunities and restrictions available to us, and as a call for particular forms of commitment. Our loves are molded to match those of our families and neighbors. And the "neighbors" are not only our immediate community, but also the community transmitted to us through media of literature and film. Intimacy that deviates from the general societal orientation must seek new contexts for its expression. For example, homosexuals tend to develop their own societal orientation—and their own literary references—for defining commitments.

Gadlin's chapter focuses on societal orientations (see also Kanter, 1972). Although he does not discuss commitment specifically, Gadlin implies that it reflects the particular social order in which it is embedded. Thus, in Puritan society domestic harmony is a facet of societal stability, and love is a facet of social duty; commitment to domestic harmony and to love of one's spouse is an integral response to the Puritan's social context. Intimacy fits with and is defined by what is demanded by the social order. Historical changes in forms of commitment are, Gadlin implies, "tied to the changing needs of the economic domain" (p. 65).

In concluding this section, I want to note again that what I have here called the societal orientation is part of our everyday, ordinary experience. We tend to see the personal as part of us and the societal as outside us—as imposed on our individual uniqueness. I believe that this view is a characteristic of the dialectic conflicts of our own era rather than a necessary perspective of realities. I shall say more of this below.

Here I wish only to emphasize that—whatever the realities—we see relationship, and specifically commitment, as part of the *social* structure of our lives. Whether we identify with, comply with, or resist the context set by our society, that context is an orientation from which we and others view and judge our own experiences.

The Interpersonal Orientation   Both personal and societal perspectives have their source in interpersonal face-to-face experience. The process by which interpersonal experience is transformed to a societal orientation is called socialization (cf. Berger & Luckmann, 1967); the process by which interpersonal experience is transformed to a personal orientation is called identity formation (cf. Erikson, 1963). The transformations of interpersonal events to form individual and societal orientations have been subject to considerable commentary and research. The orientation which is specifically interpersonal—and which shares experiential reality with the other orientations—has served as a theme of legends, plays, and novels. With some exceptions—by psychotherapist-investigators primarily—it has rarely been a field for scientific inquiry.

The interpersonal orientation views events from the stance of a face-to-face group. Within the multiple possibilities for such groupings my focus here is on the intimate dyad and particularly, though not exclusively, on the dyadic relationship which includes a strong sexual component.[11] The development of such a relationship toward an interpersonal orientation follows a sequential course,[12] including the establishment of a cycle of togetherness and apartness, a progressive linkage of verbal and nonverbal communications, a reduction of spheres of privacy, an increasing facilitation of the other's transactions with the environment. Davis (1973) suggests that this sequence is irreversible, although it may be disrupted at any point and the relationship may disintegrate. The culmination of the sequence is an intersubjectivity through which individual boundaries are transformed.

[11]Lynn Hoffman, in discussion, suggested that every dyad requires a third party for its existence and that the basic unit for analysis of close relationships is a three-person group.

[12]Davis (1973) in suggesting a science of intimate relations uses the name "philemics" for the study of behaviors through which two interacting individuals construct and communicate an intimate relation. He describes successive steps in the development of intimacy, the risks and complications these entail, and the course of dissolution of relationships. Some of my comments that follow derive from his analysis.

The intersubjectivity that emerges from continuing face-to-face interaction yields a conjoint interpersonal orientation. In this orientation, intimates "share in each other's virtues and successes . . . [and] become implicated in each other's vices and defeats" (Davis, 1973, p. 202). Moreover, experience is transmuted through a new identity as a couple.[13] From this context of the couple, commitment is not the expression of a personal or societal need but rather a mutual orientation toward the relationship itself. In a study of couples judged by their community as especially loving, Strauss (1974) finds that these generally long-married partners refer spontaneously to "working at" their relationship; the "couple identity . . . [has] its own existence, almost like a third party in the relationship" (p. 296). The commitment of these couples was not to exchanges of resources as individuals but to the larger unit that constituted their mutual relation.

In its most vital, impassioned phase, the interpersonal orientation transmutes individual experience. It selects out and amplifies some personal components and attenuates others. It not only constructs a new reality, but it rewrites memory. A past gesture, a word said, takes on an altered meaning in the aura of love (and when love disintegrates the appeal of a still-involved partner, "Do you remember when we . . . ?" no longer meets with a once affectively shared memory). Such transmutations are similar to religious conversions (James, 1903). In the intense close relationship the commitment to an interpersonal orientation alters past and current individual and societal orientations. A new self is discovered or liberated through the relationship, and the world too may bear a different visage. True, these effects may be transitory. But even this recognition would probably not reduce the seductive power of the intense relationship (cf. Lewis, 1960, pp. 158–159).

A relationship that can transmute both self-perceptions and perceptions of social realities has a powerful appeal for individuals. In our own times, it is the source of attraction to arranged group experiences which offer a hidden promise of "instant intimacy." But whether the appeal is met or unmet, the experience lasting or ephemeral, is, I believe, secondary to the importance of recognizing its presence as an orientation through which an intimate "we" transmutes both "I" and "it."

[13] The reality of the couple as a differentiable unit is demonstrated statistically in Raush et al. (1974). That the couple or family represents a Gestalt that is more than the sum of its individual members is the basis for conception and practice in family therapy (see esp. Minuchin, 1974).

Although this orientation is perhaps most visible in aspects of erotic love, it is not limited to the sexual relationship. Buber (1923) gives it far broader reference in his analysis of the I-Thou relation as an essential human—even if inevitably fragile and impermanent—orientation to fellow human beings, to nature, and to God. He distinguishes the I-Thou orientation from fusion, in that in the former the individuality of the other is recognized, confirmed, and enhanced, rather than ignored, denied, and diminished. Graziadei (1976), using therapist and client diaries, finds an evolving progression of relational structures in intensive psychotherapy. The development is from *intentionality*, an inward direction of self to other in which attitudes and feelings are hidden; to *intending the other*, a reaching out, dominated, however, by the communicated content; to *revelation*, in which the whole being is expressed and in which there is an organic wholeness between person and message; to *union*, in which partners experience equality and are joined side-by-side toward a common task; to *love*, in which there is a full response of each to the wholeness and intrinsic worth of the other.

In terms of analysis and research we know all too little about conditions for the development, maintenance, and dissolution of interpersonal orientations. Nor do we have sufficiently detailed mappings of such orientations, nor are their effects on actions clearly explicated. Furthermore, the distinctions between the position of a relational "we-ness" and symbiotic fusion or narcissistic projection are less than fully clear (see Karpel, 1976).

Part 3: The Dialectic among Orientations

Conjunctions Only at rare moments in our lives with others do we find complete congruence among personal, interpersonal, and societal orientations. At such times, individual roles and status are diffused in the service of an ideal, intimacy is in the sharing of that ideal, and at least some social unit is representative of the ideal. The ideal may be as simple as a new project or a new club, or it may be a religious, political, or social movement. A unity of purpose and conviction reflects the congruence among the three orientations. Most often the congruence fades rapidly: individual rights are reasserted; intimacy forms coalitions; and the social unit becomes fragmented.[14]

[14]Responses to disasters such as earthquakes or bombings seem to show similar characteristics: a loosening and rearrangement of boundaries to meet the crisis, followed by the reaffirmation of old boundaries.

Congruence among personal, interpersonal, and societal orientations is even more rare in history. Again, such conjunctions seem to occur only in the early stages of religious or social movements.[15] Modern China may represent a current example: observers' reports (Kessen et al., 1974) suggest a striking congruence in goals and attitudes of individuals, families, and social institutions; all three orientations seem to reflect—and be isomorphic with—a single encompassing ideological structure.

Disjunctions between Personal and Societal Orientations   Disjunctions among the different orientations are more common. Such disjunctions are the source of myth and literature. A typical theme is that of a struggle between a personal orientation—represented in the hero—and a societal orientation. In Greek myth and drama, the individual asserts his personal autonomy, transgressing against the gods. In subsequent centuries, the symbol of society shifts from that of a deity or deities and comes to be represented by symbols of class structure—religious hierarchy, feudal nobility, landed gentry, merchant, industrial entrepreneur, and, perhaps today, managerial bureaucracy.

The individual's transgression may have tragic consequences—as in Greek drama or as for Emma Bovary—or it may be resolved happily— the hero justified in the plaudits of the crowd. In the idealized synthesis, a new coalescence is established between person and society: the hero, changed through his trials, returns to found a new social order.

The dialectic between personal and societal orientations seems to concern primarily matters of power and status. But it also has ramifications for ethics and theology, as well as for politics. That theme is too broad to pursue here, but a brief tabulation of some of these extensions leads us to the following confrontations, all of which have interpersonal consequences:[16]

Societal		Personal
Duty	vs.	Grace
Order	vs.	Chaos
Responsibility	vs.	Freedom
Rational	vs.	Mystical

[15]Most often there is also an external, identifiable enemy of the movement.

[16]The dialectic and some of these ramifications are illustrated in the powerful dialogues of such works as: Dostoevsky's *Brothers Karamazov*, Shaw's *Saint Joan*, Mann's *Magic*

Interpersonal and Personal Orientations   If we seem to have wandered from our topic of the close relationship, our purpose has been to find a path for discussing dialectical issues of the interpersonal orientation. For from the points of view of both person and society the intimate dyad occupies a peculiarly ambiguous ground. Let us first consider intimacy from the standpoint of the personal orientation.

From a personal perspective, intimacy is often seen as a threat to individual autonomy, and autonomy and intimacy are often thought of as opposite ends on a continuum of self versus mutual involvement. This image, of relationship in conflict with individual expression, meshes with a frontier-oriented individualism and male fears of encumbrance, as described by Douvan; it also fits with current emphases on self-growth.

But dyadic intimacy is not always seen as opposed to individual autonomy. From the personal orientation of its participants, intimacy offers an expansion of individual resources; the relationship yields sexual, social, and economic benefits to the individual partners. Moreover, as discussed earlier in part 2, the intimate relationship also offers an arena for self-discovery and for transcendance of personal limitations.

Furthermore, developmental considerations demand rejection of the idea of autonomy and intimacy as polar opposites. Autonomy itself is founded on relationship: For the child to develop a sense of autonomy—a sense of self as an individual—a caring relationship with a trustworthy adult is essential. Similarly, autonomy is a prerequisite for adult intimacy;[17] intimacy that is other than projective identification or symbiotic fusion requires partners who are separate individuals and who are capable of recognizing the other's individuality. Developmentally, personal autonomy and interpersonal intimacy are necessarily intertwined.

Viewed from a personal perspective, the interpersonal orientation thus presents a dilemma. Intimacy can be in conflict with autonomy, but it can also share its goals. Personal and interpersonal contexts can be either conjunctive or disjunctive. Their mesh or clash varies with historical and cultural differences. But it also varies with individual and

---

Mountain, Koestler's *Darkness at Noon,* Orwell's *1984.* These issues are also the subject of biblical and other religious legends, and they are the preoccupations of philosophers dating at least from Plato.

[17]Ryder in discussion emphasized this point. See Erikson (1963) for fuller explication.

relationship life cycles, and with individual and class differences in goals and expectations of self and relationship. These points suggest issues for research. The analysis moreover suggests that, instead of focusing on autonomy and intimacy as opposites, research should examine the conditions for their conjunction or disjunction.

Interpersonal and Societal Orientations   The close relationship is no less complicated from a societal perspective. On one hand, the love story has universal appeal—"all the world loves a lover." Eros transcends selfish desire; it brings out noble and hidden virtues; in our secular times it is seen as a source of salvation. Moreover, its process culminates in the induction of the intimate pair into a societal mainstream. Ideally, the loving pair is tamed, domesticated, socialized, responsible, and ready for consistent work and the rearing of a new generation.

But Eros has a double meaning that makes it not only attractive but also dangerous to the larger society. If its one side represents life and creativity, a hope for the emergence of that which is new and better, its other side represents irrational passion and a capacity for disrupting the normal order of events. Bion (1961) has noted the fascination that the pairing process has for any group that is having difficulty in its task; it is fancied that the pair will rescue the group from all its problems. Bion points to this as an illusory assumption—a false hope which distracts the group from its real work.

Creative or disruptive, the transcendent potential of the intimate relationship can be a force for social change. To risk an analogy: Biologically, from an evolutionary standpoint, the advantage of sexual as compared to asexual reproduction is that it produces diversity; although diversity may yield a higher proportion of error, it allows for the development of variations that adapt to altered ecological circumstances. So, too, the interpersonal may represent an aspect of what may be called adaptive probabilism (see Raush et al., 1974). That is, the intimate pair may be a medium through which outmoded societal orientations are altered.

Whether the potential of the interpersonal orientation becomes realized or unrealized, whether its effects serve creatively or destructively, are matters or conditions that we know all too little about. As with the personal, relations between interpersonal and societal orientations may be either conjunctive or disjunctive; intimacy, either generally or specifically, may either mesh or clash with its societal context. Their interplay, how one influences and alters the other, is also a matter for research. Gadlin's chapter is an example of such research and is discussed below. But first I want to examine briefly dialectical possibilities of the interpersonal orientation.

Dialectics of the Interpersonal Orientation

Interpersonal and personal versus societal orientation The interpersonal orientation, as noted, can play a shifting dialectical position. Thus, it can coalesce with a personal orientation to test, attack, or modulate a contemporary societal view. For example, Romeo and Juliet, in their individual and their joint passions, test the boundary between the Montague and Capulet clans. Their relationship serves—at the end of Shakespeare's play—to dissolve clan boundaries. The transcendent power of intimacy is demonstrated—but also its dangers: the two lovers must die to achieve the social transformation. Other legends and historical romances—such as Tristram and Iseult, or Héloise and Abelard—serve in their tragic consequences to illustrate the dangers of and to the intimate pair in their threat to the social order. In our own day, also, the loyalty between intimates is felt as a threat to the contemporary societal orientation. Totalitarian regimes are correct, in a sense, in their suspicion of the disruptiveness and revolutionary potential of interpersonal intimacy. Love joined with power is a formidable combatant.

Interpersonal and societal versus personal orientation The interpersonal can, however, also ally with the societal in opposition to the personal orientation. Legend also illustrates the call to the comforts of intimacy, to integration with the social milieu—Odysseus, the wanderer, longing for and returning home. As Gadlin illustrates, intimacy has often served society by domesticating, or providing an outlet for, individual impulse.

Interpersonal versus personal and societal orientation In a third dialectical position, the interpersonal stands against a coalition between the personal and the societal. The frontier mentality, described by Douvan, of the American males who headed west, deserting wives and children, expressed an individual impulse for autonomy which was fostered by societal goals of conquest and exploitation. In that dialectical conflict, interpersonal intimacy was the loser.

Whether it is inevitable that the interpersonal realm lose out when it is aligned against personal and societal orientations, I do not know. One may, however, note a type of popular novel and film that has it otherwise. The plot goes something like this: Society is represented by a given group: a police force, a school or hospital, a newspaper, corporation, a political party, or even—as in some science fiction—a national or world government. More rarely the societal stance is indicated by a general atmosphere. The image of society is initially presented as corrupt or evil. In its simpler versions, the plot begins with the hero fully identified with the societal stance. That is, the hero's personal strivings mesh with those of the group. At the next stage of the plot, however, love enters. A struggle is engaged. The outcome of this stage is the hero's transformation; through the transcendence of intimacy, the hero becomes a changed person. Now the dialectic shifts: a new coalition forms between the interpersonal and a transformed personal orientation against the societal. The couple unite to reject the initial societal orientation or, better yet, to transform it. In less sophisticated presentations, the "bad" company or the "bad" politicians are overturned, thus bringing about a new societal orientation which harmonizes with the interpersonal and the now-changed personal.

My point in detailing this theme is not to suggest that it represents real outcomes. The myth that love can both transform the person and change society may be unfounded in the world of real events. It may serve as an illusory sop to maintain the existing order. Nonetheless, the very ubiquity of this myth suggests the power that people ascribe to love as a source of change. Moreover, that the myth itself has "real" effects on behavior is demonstrated by the appeal of evangelical movements which offer love—though they define it somewhat differently—as a way of changing one's self and one's world. It is surprising that social research has neglected questions of how love transforms, or fails to transform, images of self and of society.

Dialectic alignments and shifts are reflected in the changing conceptions of intimate relationships in American history. With Gadlin's analysis as a base, we may examine some of these changes, noting the balances among personal, interpersonal, and societal orientations.

Part 4: Dialectic of Intimacy in American History

The Colonial Era   The intimacy of the colonial era seems alien to our current conceptions. Can we, as did American colonials, conceive of love as obedience to God and as duty to a community that represents

God's chosen order? To comprehend the meaning of intimacy at that very different period (and very different culture) requires that we capture not only the earlier economic and social structure but also the sense of the very dust in the streets, the sounds, the smells, the structure of buildings and rooms, the different sense of distance and of daily time and of what is private and what public, the fragility of life and omnipresence of death, the permanence of God's moral order and his watchfulness.

From our contemporary distance, the colonial conception of intimacy reflects predominantly a societal orientation. For the colonials, intimacy served God and a clearly articulated social order. Moreover, Gadlin's description suggests that the colonial era was characterized by a rare degree of congruence among personal, interpersonal, and societal orientations. Community, family, and individual life all reflect the same pattern: As God knows and judges all souls, the community knows and judges all actions; as God is first righteous, and then loving, so is husband and father. Sex, socialized into this pattern, is seen as virtuous—Gadlin notes the charming term "felicity."

It was the unsocialized, individualized sexual passion that was sinful. A threat to the dialectic balance seems, for the colonials, to have been the assertion of individualism. That side of man and woman was believed perverse and in need of control. Perverse autonomy was embodied in the Devil, who would subvert God's order by supplanting obedience with willfulness. Witchery, in that sense, was the expression of individual willfulness.

The colonial conception of intimacy seems reflected in the dances of the era. The couple performs a set pattern in the context of the group. Couples join and separate, but the pattern is fixed and it is the community that surrounds and controls the dance. Individual skill and grace may be called for but never individual self-expression (see Damon, 1957).

The Jacksonian Era   The pulls and strains of an emerging industrial capitalism in the Jacksonian era are reflected in changed conceptions and changed behavior in interpersonal relationships. As work and home become separate spheres of existence, relationships become fragmented. At the same time, however, the loss of a cohesive community places an increased burden of maintaining cohesion on the nuclear family. Both entrepreneurial enterprise and frontier development promote an individualistic personal orientation that is opposed to and threatened by close relationships (see Douvan, this volume). At the same time, however, the alienation produced by increasingly meaningless work fosters the appeal of intimacy as sanctuary. Thus, the Jacksonian era suggests uncertainty and confusion in the dialectic of intimacy. The personal orientation seems to involve both attraction to and rejection of interpersonal closeness; the societal orientation seems both to promote and to discourage intimacy.

In individual psychology, ambivalences are often projected externally by a form of "splitting." For example, a sexual ambivalence may be expressed by dividing women into two classes—the "good" and the "bad." The dialectics of the Jacksonian era, as indicated by Gadlin, suggest such an attempt. Work and frontier exploration become in a sense sexualized in the romanticization—which still has appeals today—of a rugged, competitive individualism. From this point of view, intimacy is seen as threatening. On the other side, there is also a romanticization—unknown to colonial times—of the intimate relationship as an idealized sanctuary and as a source of social stability. The family becomes "good"; sex becomes "bad."

The loss of an integrated societal orientation is perhaps reflected in changes in the dance. The formalities of popular dance structures begin to disintegrate in the Jacksonian era. The dance "caller" appears for the first time. The once fixed sequence of patterns is no longer given communally, and it is the "caller" who sets the sequence (see Damon, 1957).

The Progressive Era   The loss of a controlling social community, the dependence on formal institutions for conveying and maintaining social relations, the alienation from work increase during the time that Gadlin has labeled the progressive era. Decreasing economic opportunities reduce the emphasis on entrepreneurial initiative and promote increased emphasis on intimacy. Since personal independence no longer supports—and indeed may threaten—societal goals, sex can reemerge as a conscious aspect of intimacy. In the progressive era, sex thus serves both "self-expression"—an emerging aspect of the personal orientation—and intimacy—which becomes increasingly defined as dyadic rather than as familial or communal. The personal orientation becomes represented in the myth of "free" marital choice; the interpersonal in the myth that relationships will provide both romantic sexual fulfillment and rational companionship; the societal in the myth of male "instrumental," executive activity as contrasted to female "expressive," family-oriented activity.

In this era, the dance becomes that of a couple as the unit. Each couple dances in close physical contact, apart from other couples, and with little or no sense of social community. The male leads, the female follows. The dance steps, however, are patterned to the music, and some elements of a formal sequence are maintained.[18] I call attention to Gadlin's subtitle for the progressive era: in contrast to "Formal Intimacy" for the colonial era and "Spiritual Intimacy" for the Jacksonian era, his heading here is just "Intimacy."

The Contemporary Experience   If the colonial era is too distant for our proper comprehension, the present time is too close. Nonetheless, from the base of what Gadlin calls the progressive era some shifts can be noted.

Consider first the personal orientation. Although Gadlin says that the progressive era is characterized by a personal goal of "self-fulfillment," I believe that this term is misleading. Personal gratification, personal achievement, personal expression, self-awareness, and self-determination of choices all contribute to images of self in the progressive era. But the strivings were directed less toward "self-fulfilment" than toward a broadening of roles and greater "self-expression."

Notions of self-fulfillment and self-actualization are more characteristic of present-day personal images, in which the self is seen as a kind of internal homunculus, demanding release from social bonds so that it can grow and become actualized. The self is not only to be "expressed," but it is now obligated to induce its own development.[19] Moreover, the failure of the self to "grow" is now cause for guilt.

Before turning to the interpersonal realm, let us consider the societal

[18]As the dance steps are structured and sequenced to the music, so too there is a structure and sequence to the close relationship in the progressive era. If some steps have dropped out—the formal introduction of partners, the chaperoned courtship, parental sanctioning, the formal proposal—other rituals remain—the engagement and its ring, the wedding that unites two family groups and signifies social ties by the formalities of dress, ritual, and liturgy. Added to these is an elaborately sequenced pattern of "dating."

[19]Kanter, in discussion, termed this nicely: "the discovery of adulthood." Her implication is that adulthood is no longer seen as a fixed condition but "is discovered" as an unstable stage undergoing change. If persons are in a fluid process of change, then relationships, as she suggested, must tend to become less permanent.

orientation. Although attenuated, the image of the close relationship was relatively unambiguous in the progressive era. The goal of heterosexual intimacy was marriage—a happy and, above all, a stable marriage. For marriage counselors and researchers through the 1930s, the forties, and even the fifties, stability was the main index of marital satisfaction. This is no longer true. No longer is there one single societal standard for intimate relationships. Rather, there are multiple standards. The societal orientation becomes a Babel of voices. Contemporary novelists and playwrights are hard put to find themes of transgression which arouse the modern audience. Themes of adultery and homosexuality have lost their shock value. To explore the social limits of intimacy, modern authors look increasingly to such themes as pedophilia and incest (e.g., in Nabokov's novels). Increasingly, as Gadlin implies, the only social sin with respect to relationships is bad technique.

Turning to the interpersonal orientation, we again see changes. Sexuality, legitimized during the progressive era, now becomes separated from intimacy and becomes defused and "technicalized."[20] The burdens on the intimate pair continue to increase. Each couple must decide for itself between marriage and just living together; it must shape its own rituals, its attitudes toward stability and change, its own stand toward exclusiveness and inclusiveness vis-à-vis other relationships. And whatever its "commitment," the current interpersonal relationship must include a commitment to continuing negotiation.

The traditional marital vow—"to love and to cherish" the partner ("to obey" and "till death us do part" having now dropped out)—is transformed from its earlier meaning. In the current interpersonal orientation, "to love" means to promote the other's personal growth. Although this definition of love appears viable, we must recognize that it represents a new orientation toward intimacy.

The current conflict, then, seems to be between personal and interpersonal orientations. Present-day films, plays, and novels suggest that it is the personal orientation that is now the hero-protagonist: the

[20]Rossi, in discussion, called attention to current changes in women's perspectives paralleling men's perspectives. For women, as for men, she suggested, sexual intimacy now comes to precede rather than follow social intimacy. The improvement in birth control methods and changes in legal and social sanctions, deriving from the decreasing economic functions and values of the nuclear family, contribute to the perspective on sexuality as self-expressive and recreational.

most common theme seems to be that of "becoming oneself," within or against the ties of intimacy.[21] In this emphasis on the individual there is a resemblance to the frontier mentality. Now, though, the conceptions are shared by men and women, the frontier is wholly subjective, and its boundaries are diffuse.

We are, as has been noted throughout these chapters, in a time of rapid change, and any description of the current situation is apt to be outmoded by the time it is published. I have emphasized the fragmentation of the societal and the strength of the personalistic that seem to characterize the contemporary dialectic of intimacy. Nevertheless, there are countertrends. For example, the search for a sense of community is strong among young people. Moreover, although the stability of close relationships is put into question, the responsibilities of intimacy have never before been taken more seriously in that a concern for the other's psychological well-being and personal development has replaced economic and role functionalism. There are probably fewer "empty shell" relationships—and here I include friendships as well as sexual partnerships. There are also voices that go counter to the prevailing technological orientation described by Gadlin—for example, his own.

To return to the dance: Today's formation is still one of pairs, and the music provides the background. There is no defined sequence of steps; the partners are in minimal and momentary contact with each other, and each does as he or she wishes; the emphasis is on individual autonomy of action while meeting in transit. There are, however, countertrends, expressed in revivals of folk, square, and contra-dances and in the strong attraction these communal dances have for many young people.

Part 5: Internalization, Externalization, and Intimacy

In referring to personal, interpersonal, and societal forces as "orientations," my intent has been to focus on the positions from which we view relationships, whether our own or those of others. I have suggested these orientations as coexisting perspectives which sometimes coalesce and sometimes compete with one another. Which orientation dominates is partly a matter of the historical and cultural circumstances

[21]Even the commune, as Kanter (1972) notes, becomes used as a context for self-actualization.

that we are born into. But only partly. Within a specific relationship, or within an individual's life span of relationships, orientations shift in dominance and alignments change. We know all too little about these movements—what influences us to see our relationships now according to one set of terms, now according to another set. The dialectic, discussed above, describes some directions of change in our experience and conception of relationships. It says little about *how* change occurs. To touch on that topic requires some comment on "objective" and "subjective" reality, and on internalization and externalization.

"Objective" and "Subjective" Reality My emphasis on "orientation" as psychological perspective does not imply that reality is entirely within us or is only what we ourselves perceive. There is an objective social order that shapes our societal orientations; there are real others with whom we share interpersonal orientations; and our physical and psychological boundaries as persons are real. But although the social order is real, it is a human product, brought into being by human activity; the interpersonal realm is similarly a product of ongoing human interaction; and our personal selves are constructions of the meanings we give to the flux of experience. The "objective" is continually created and recreated by the "subjective" and vice versa. To quote Berger and Luckmann (1967): "symmetry between objective and subjective reality is never a static once-for-all state of affairs. It must always be produced and reproduced in *actu*" (p. 134).[22] Changes in orientation occur when what is "objective" becomes "subjective"—that is, internalized—or when what is "subjective" becomes "objective"— that is, externalized.

Internalization and Change In internalization, something that was initially not "me" becomes a part of "me." Commitment, thus, can be thought of as a process of internalization. In committing myself to another—or to a group, a concept, an ideal—that which I previously considered external to me becomes an integral part of me; and what happens to that "other" is no longer "outside" me.[23] Boundaries between inner and outer have become redefined. A new Gestalt is

[22]The above paragraph and much of what follows are strongly influenced by Berger & Luckmann (1967). See esp. pp. 53–67 and pp. 129–138.

[23]This is coordinate with Kanter's (1972) notion of commitment as a systems concept which relates personal motives to a social unit.

formed in which the meanings of events and acts are transformed.

As suggested above, commitment need not be solely personal. When intimates live together and are involved in continuing interaction, they must coorient to issues they share in common—their own relationship, relationships with others, and so on. The dyadic partnership thus becomes a fertile ground for creating joint commitments and for developing common internalized orientations.

Externalization and Change Externalization—as used in this context—is the obverse of internalization: something that was initially seen as a part of "me" becomes "not me." A simple illustration may be taken from interviews with newlywed couples some fifteen years ago (Raush et al., 1974). When these couples were asked how they decided about handling relations with friends or how they decided about dealing with parents, our questions were seen as reasonable and discussable. When, however, the couples were asked how they decided about who cooks, the response in most instances was a blank, confused stare. Clearly, fifteen years ago the decision as to who cooks was not conscious. Female responsibility for cooking was part of a social orientation that was, for most couples of that time, isomorphic with interpersonal and personal orientations. Today, the question is subject to conscious consideration, discussion, and negotiation. The issue is externalized rather than seen as part of the internal female "me."

When discrepancies among personal, interpersonal, and societal orientations become massive, that which was formerly taken for granted is apt to come into question. Disjunctions among orientations can thus lead to a "raising of consciousness." What was formerly not conscious now becomes objectified; what was formerly internal is externalized. In the treatment of an issue as an objective problem change can evolve. A personal, interpersonal, or societal orientation may be modified and new commitments undertaken.[24]

[24]One may compare this dialectic with descriptions of the psychoanalytic process. In psychoanalytic therapy a problem cannot be dealt with if it is entirely projected or externalized—for example, "It's all my wife's (my boss's, the system's) fault." What is seen wholly as a result of external forces uninfluenceable by actions of the self is not subject to analytic exploration. Similarly, that which is seen as an integral, essential part of self, as something that cannot be questioned—for example, "my kindheartedness," "my bad temper," etc.—is not subject to analysis. Both the completely ego-syntonic and the completely ego-alien are therapeutically unanalyzable. The issue for the analyst (and the patient) is that of maintaining a balance between the fully externalized and the fully

A continuing close relationship involves differences in viewpoints, and through these differences partners may come to question what was formerly taken for granted. In this process that which was internalized as characterizing "us" may come to be seen as no longer valid. The outcome may be dissolution of the relationship or a modification of former orientations and commitments.

The Intimate Relationship   An intimate relationship will partake of both processes. The dialectic balance between the two processes will vary with specific times and specific relationships. That is, two sources of variation have been implied above: Internalization will be favored in periods of congruence among personal, interpersonal, and societal orientations within and between partners; externalization will be favored when there are disjunctions among these orientations, either within or between partners.

By virtue of its physical immediacy and continuity, the intimate relationship tends to force internalizations and externalizations that might not otherwise occur. In this way it becomes a powerful medium for both continuity and change. Through the process of internalization, the dyad can form a stable set of orientations and commitments for its own continuity and for the socialization of a new generation. Through the process of externalization, the dyad can move beyond the limits of each individual partner's upbringing toward new orientations and commitments, changing its own course and, in turn, the course of a new generation.

Conclusion

My final remarks can be brief. I have suggested here that some of the confusions about the close relationship—particularly those concerning the influences of internal and external constraints—are clarified by thinking of the close relationship as process rather than as state. This process involves a dialectic among personal, interpersonal, and societal

---

internalized. The analyst must deal first with those aspects of the patient's self that are seen by the latter as painful—as unwanted parts; when these aspects are no longer problematic, other issues may emerge. The patient must be able to maintain an equilibrium between experiencing and observing the events under analysis. In the direction toward change both patient and analyst are involved in a process of ever-changing balances between internalization and externalization.

orientations to the relationship, and a dialectic between internalization and externalization. The outcomes of these two dialectics vary with historical and cultural circumstances, and within the life course of particular relationships. I have pointed to the influence that personal and societal orientations have on enactments of intimacy; but I have also emphasized the special power of the interpersonal in transforming personal and societal orientations.

In attempting to de-reify the close relationship by analyzing it as an ongoing process, I fear that I have not wholly avoided the dangers of other reifications. For example, my reference to a "societal orientation" may suggest a disconnected entity rather than one that is continually reconstructed by human activity. Furthermore, reference to "a" personal, interpersonal, or social orientation suggests falsely the image of singular, undifferentiated structures. I hope that the reader is not misled but bears in mind that "a" personal orientation, for example, is itself constructed of subunits and that parts of the personal perspective may be congruent or disjunctive with one another. Thus, within each orientation there is also an ongoing dialectic which for present purposes has been ignored. Discussion of process, as has often been noted, suffers particularly from limitations of discourse and language.[25]

I have suggested that the dialectic processes discussed above are directed toward greater isomorphy among orientations. Put more simply, as human beings we are continually involved in the effort to pull together the diverse forces that impinge on our lives and become parts of the ways we look at ourselves and our worlds. In that effort the intimate relationship plays an important role. Conceptual analyses of close relationships, research noted or suggested throughout this volume, show recognition of that importance. The volume itself can be seen as a dialectic engagement of orientations, directed—in its individual contributions and its whole—toward integrating the diversities and complexities of intimacy.

References

Barker, R. G. *Ecological psychology.* Stanford, Calif.: Stanford University Press, 1968.

Berger, P. L., & Luckmann, T. *The social construction of reality.* New York: Anchor Books, 1967.

Bion, W. R. *Experiences in groups.* New York: Basic Books, 1961.

---

[25] I am indebted to Jack Hewitt for his thoughts on these issues.

Buber, M. *I and thou* (1923). 2nd ed. New York: Scribner's, 1958.

Damon, S. F. The history of square dancing. From *Proceedings of the American Antiquarian Society*. Barre, Mass.: Barre Gazette, 1957.

Davis, M. S. *Intimate relations*. New York: Free Press, 1973.

Erikson, E. H. *Childhood and society* (2nd ed.). New York: Norton, 1963.

Graziadei, J. M. Partners in journey: A dialectic of psychotherapy. Ph.D. dissertation, University of Massachusetts, Amherst, 1976.

Haley, J. *Strategies of psychotherapy*. New York: Grune & Stratton, 1963.

James, W. *Varieties of religious experience* (1903). New York: Macmillan, 1972.

Jourard, S. M. *Self-disclosure: An experimental analysis of the transparent self*. New York: Wiley-Interscience, 1971.

Kanter, R. M. *Commitment and community*. Cambridge: Harvard University Press, 1972.

Karpel, M. Individuation: From fusion to dialogue. *Family Process*, 1976, *15*, 65–82.

Kessen, W.; Bronfenbrenner, U.; Stevenson, H.; Caldwell, B.; Yarrow, M.; & Maccoby, E. Children of China: Report of a visit. Symposium presented at the American Psychological Association Annual Meeting, New Orleans, August 30, 1974.

Lederer, W. J., & Jackson, D. D. *The mirages of marriage*. New York: W. W. Norton, 1968.

Lewis, C. S. *The four loves*. New York: Harcourt Brace Jovanovich, 1960.

Minuchin, S. *Families and family therapy*. Cambridge: Harvard University Press, 1974.

Raush, H. L.; Barry, W. A.; Hertel, R. K.; & Swain, M. A. *Communication, conflict, and marriage*. San Francisco: Jossey-Bass, 1974.

Sarason, S. B. *The psychological sense of community*. San Francisco: Jossey-Bass, 1974.

Strauss, E. *Couples in love*. Ph.D. dissertation, University of Massachusetts, Amherst, 1974.

Thibaut, J. W., & Kelley, H. H. *The social psychology of groups*. New York: Wiley, 1959.

Author Index

CONTRIBUTORS

Elizabeth Douvan, Professor of Psychology, University of Michigan

Howard Gadlin, Associate Professor of Psychology, University of Massachusetts, Amherst

Harold H. Kelley, Professor of Psychology, University of California at Los Angeles

George Levinger, Professor of Psychology, University of Massachusetts, Amherst

David H. Olson, Professor of Family Studies, University of Minnesota

Harold L. Raush, Professor of Psychology, University of Massachusetts, Amherst

Paul C. Rosenblatt, Professor of Family Social Science and of Psychology, University of Minnesota

Library of Congress Cataloging in Publication Data

Symposium on Priorities in Research on Close
 Relationships, Amherst, Mass., 1974.
 Close relationships.

 Bibliography: p.
 Includes index.
 1. Intimacy (Psychology) — Congresses.
I. Douvan, Elizabeth Ann Malcolm, 1926–
II. Levinger, George Klaus, 1927–   III. Raush,
Harold L.   IV. Title.
BF575.I5S9   1974   301.11'2   77-900
ISBN 0-87023-238-X